bridge between worlds

Ezra Pound

Letters

John Theobald

edited by Donald Pearce
and Herbert Schneidau

BLACK SWAN BOOKS

First edition
Published by
BLACK SWAN BOOKS Ltd.
P. O. Box 327
REDDING RIDGE, CT 06876
ISBN 0-933806-02-7

Contents

ACKNOWLEDGEMENTS

We thank the following organizations and individuals for assistance in making this volume possible: the Friends of the University of California, Santa Barbara, Library for their purchase of the letters; Olga Ignon, assistant librarian, for her initiative; Chris Brun, head of Special Collections, for various courtesies connected with the preparation of the manuscript; James Laughlin, publisher of New Directions Publishing Corp. for numerous kindnesses extended to us in the book's early stages; the executors of the Ezra Pound Literary Property Trust for permission to publish the letters; the Research Committee, University of California, Santa Barbara, for financial assistance; Amy Nathanson and Merrie Appleman for their careful transcripts of passages that were often very difficult; John Walsh, publisher of Black Swan Books, for his valuable and persistent efforts in the preparation of Notes and Glossary. One could not ask for more courtesy than we have had from John Theobald, whose spirited letters we have found refreshing, as they surely must once have proved to "the noble prisoner in the dippydip." Deletions of passages in the letters are indicated by dots.

Donald Pearce
Herbert Schneidau

PUBLISHER'S NOTE

In these letters from St. Elizabeths, Pound speaks his mind directly and unstintingly—recalling his oft-quoted phrase from Rémy de Gourmont: "to express frankly what one thinks—sole pleasure of a writer." Not only does Pound speak forthrightly in these letters, but vehemently as well. Transgressed are the Confucian *dicta* of decorum and balance; a just measure in statement, a holding fast to gradations, become betrayed by violence in language. It is only after his release from St. Elizabeths that Pound is able to write (in a letter to Archibald MacLeish) with calmness restored: "Forgive me for about 80% of the violent things I have said about some of your friends . . . it is probably too late to retract them. . . . Violent language is an error. I did not get full of Agassiz. That might have saved me. Whether my errors can be useful to others, God knows."

These are letters issuing from a man *in extremis*. For Pound they act as a "bridge between worlds," offering him an opportunity to both communicate and educate, in the hope of having an *effect* on the world outside the walls. An opportunity to influence the direction of the teaching of literature *via* Theobald's projected textbook: never completed, the idea formed for Pound the germinal seed for *Confucius to Cummings*.

Pound actively responded to the opportunity provided by Theobald by offering an agenda. Ideas, names and themes are presented in the letters in staccato fashion, much as notes in the arpeggiated chords of a Mozart concerto. The tempo is always rapid: *vivace, presto, allegro*. There can always be discerned on Pound's part a press to move on. The receiver catches what he can; for the reader who might want them, endnotes have been included at the back of the present volume. (Most certainly, Poundians do not *need* them; others less familiar with Pound's frame of reference and cast of mind might, it is hoped, find them useful.) In the apparent chaos (an impression which upon rereading dissolves further and further away) of the letters, there can be discerned a gleam of gold: an emphasis on a philosophy of light, extending from Plotinus and Proclus through John Scotus Erigena, Grosseteste and Richard of St. Victor, refracted in the mental clarity of a Confucius, a Botticelli, a Mozart, a Linnaeus, an Agassiz. In the turmoil, there endures an adherence to a central thread of order and exactitude.

These letters form a moving document, providing direct insight into Pound's consistent preoccupations. The expressions in the letters are self-revelatory—and not objective statements—of a man imprisoned, as he thought, for his honest beliefs, and evidence the torment in his mind of a wound which would not heal. Of course, the views and opinions expressed therein are by no means intended to reflect those of either the editors or the publisher: rather they are a testament to what Pound thought and felt most passionately during this last phase of his "Elizabethan period."

Acknowledgements

In preparing these letters for publication, the publisher would like first to cite the graciousness, help and encouragement of Mary de Rachewiltz, James Laughlin and Donald Gallup, and to thank them for reading through the first draft of the book and offering their comments and suggestions. Other scholars have been generous indeed in their help with regard to annotations: Marcella (Spann) Booth, William French, David Gordon, Andrew Kappel, Sanehide Kodama and René Odlin. Thanks are extended most gratefully for all their assistance; any error which might inadvertently have slipped in remains, of course, the responsibility of the publisher.

Acknowledgements for the annotations must also be made to the special issue of *Helix* (13/14), "Ezra Pound in Melbourne," edited by Les Harrop and Noel Stock, and the entire run of *Paideuma*, edited by Carroll Terrell; to the invaluable books of Pound scholarship: Donald Gallup's *Ezra Pound: A Bibliography*, second edition (referred to in the endnotes as *Gallup*) and Carroll Terrell's *A Companion to the Cantos of Ezra Pound*; to the indispensable books on Pound: Mary de Rachewiltz's *Discretions*, Noel Stock's *The Life of Ezra Pound* and Hugh Kenner's *The Pound Era*; to the extremely helpful books focused on Pound's years in St. Elizabeths: Harry Meacham's *The Caged Panther*, Eustace Mullins' *This Difficult Individual: Ezra Pound* and Michael Reck's *Ezra Pound: A Close-Up*; also to *Charles Olson & Ezra Pound*, edited by Catherine Seelye, and *An Examination of Ezra Pound*, edited by Peter Russell.

Special thanks are given to Sheri Martinelli for the frontispiece portrait of Ezra Pound.

Thanks as well are given for permission to include in the annotation excerpts from: *Edge*, granted by Noel Stock; *The Caged Panther*, granted by G. K. Hall & Co.; Ernest Hemingway, granted by Charles Scribner's Sons; William Carlos Williams, granted by New Directions Publishing Corp.; Ezra Pound, granted by the Ezra Pound Literary Property Trust and New Directions Publishing Corp. The citations for previously published material by Ezra Pound are as follows: *The Cantos* (copyright 1934, 1937, 1940, 1948, 1956, 1959, 1962, 1963, 1966, 1968 by Ezra Pound; copyright © 1972 by the Estate of Ezra Pound); *Literary Essays*, edited by T. S. Eliot (copyright 1918, 1920, 1935 by Ezra Pound); *Pavannes and Divagations* (copyright © 1958 by Ezra Pound); *Selected Prose 1909–1965*, edited by William Cookson (copyright © 1973 by the Estate of Ezra Pound); "Letter to Archibald MacLeish" in C. David Heymann, *Ezra Pound: The Last Rower* (copyright © 1976 by The Trustees of the Ezra Pound Literary Trust); *Ezra Pound Speaking*, edited by Leonard Doob (copyright © 1978 by the Ezra Pound Literary Property Trust); "Letter to Louis Zukofsky" (November 24 and 25, 1930), edited by Barry Ahearn, in *Montemora 8* (copyright © 1981 by The Trustees of the Ezra Pound Literary Property Trust); and "Letter to Wyndham Lewis," edited by Timothy Materer, in *Helix* 13/14 (copyright © 1982 The Ezra Pound Literary Property Trust).

Thanks are also personally extended to the curators and staff of The Beinecke Library, Yale University for their helpfulness and expertise in facilitating research.

Any inadvertent omissions to the above list are apologized for in advance by the publisher.

Note on the Text

As Pound used the typewriter much in the way a pianist approaches his instrument, an attempt has been made to approximate the visual appearance on the page of Pound's letters. This, of course, has not proven possible in absolutely every case. Furthermore, there has been a translation from the limited possibilities of a typewriter into the more fluid and varied opportunities offered by typesetting. Thus, underlined words have been rendered in italics; double underlined words are indicated by bold face; and triple underlining appears as italic capitals. Words originally in block letters appear in small capitals in the printed text. Handwritten inserts have been placed in the text where indicated by Pound and appear in italics within angle brackets. Even though Pound did not usually underline words and phrases from foreign languages (so numerous that it would certainly have proven a nuisance for Pound to have done so), such have been italicized in the printed text. All such typesetting translations have been practised for the purpose of clarification, since the letters are so varied in stylistic effects as to potentially overwhelm or distract the reader's glance across the page—some letters having the visual appearance of a fireworks display. What has been striven for is a reproduction in legible and pleasing form of how Pound's letters looked on the page, having in many instances striking resemblances with pages of the *Cantos*.

A minimal amount of silent emendation and deletion in the text has been exercised according to discretion. Except for extremely few instances, Pound's original spelling, spacing and punctuation has been retained, as the former reflects, in the majority of cases, puns, allusions, compound-metaphors, etc., and the latter provide keys to intonation, rhythm and emphasis.

The letters have been numbered both sequentially in a combined and intermixed sequence, and individually with regard to each author. Typed letters by Pound (all letters included in the present volume are such) are designated by TL, and signed typed letters are noted as TLS.

Notes on individual references in the letters (listed under the letter's number) and a glossary of frequently mentioned names have been provided at the end of the volume.

Pound / Theobald

Letters

All I want is a generous spirit in customs

ιst/ honest man's heart demands sane curricula

—*Canto* XCIX

Foreword

THE FOLLOWING CORRESPONDENCE with Ezra Pound was begun in April 1957 and continued on a return-mail basis for nearly eleven months. Early that year I had been working on a poetry textbook aimed at "High Placement Sections" in high schools and at one point it struck me as a good idea to ask a number of contemporary poets to indicate their own choices. I wrote to perhaps twenty poets. Some ignored my letter; some referred me to their publisher; a few offered an outright gift of a poem. Others answered my query and named a fee, in most cases disproportionate (upwards or downwards) to their talent.

Unfortunately, I seem not to have kept Pound's reply to my initial request, but it was to the effect that he hadn't written his poems for children. I remember thinking at the time, "Well, nice try, anyway," and presumably threw the letter away. Then after a minimum of delay I received another and haughtier missive: Hadn't I understood that I was being invited to correspond with him? This one I answered, and the present correspondence got underway.

My answer must have raised the possibility of using "The Goodly Fere," thus occasioning the response dated 26 April in which Pound refers to that poem as Sunday School material. Thereafter, I kept all but two of his letters. I don't know how those two got away.

The correspondence was a rough road. I am no cryptologist and at first I used to wonder whether my eminent "pen pal" was in fact a natural inmate; though actually, of course, these letters are as sharp as any previously published, simply more telegraphic. In one of my early answers, I suppose I must have protested his epistolary ellipses and abbreviations—which only prompted the *tu quoque* of 16 May.

I ought to make clear that I was not a Pound fan. I had never read the *Cantos*. And when I began to, I didn't get along too well. I'm sure I could have obtained some help from the commentators; but most of them, the "Tribe of Ez" they called themselves, "Ezroids" as Pound called them, rather reminded me of Byron's line about Coleridge: "I wish he would explain his explanation." My insufficient grounding in the works of my correspondent was a source of greater embarrassment to me than to Pound, however, who disliked sycophants.

Eliot was "Possum." It seemed to me he no longer took him very seriously, though in the matter of E.P.'s incarceration Possum had been more than kind—"at first." His religion—or religiosity— was "Possum's lousy religion." Sandburg was "Sandbag." "In Frost, yes" (commenting on one of my own rather extensive recollections of Frost during my Amherst years), "there was a mean New England streak." (If I misquote, it's not by much.) Marianne Moore was as bad as I about Jews. Neither of us seemed to understand — so he felt at that point — that good individual Jews did not alter the general problem. D.H. Lawrence, whom I had once written on, and had thought the best modern novelist, was "first among the second rate." Hemingway was "Hem," the author of what I thought a silly poem, but which Ezra had quoted (more than once, I find) with great delight. So it was not surprising that he treated with wintry silence my comparison of Hemingway's ego to a carbuncle.

The nearest he came to a literary exchange was in answer to my question of whether it was true or apocryphal that Joyce had told Yeats on the occasion of their meeting that the latter was "too old for me to help you," or some such words. I knew that Pound, having lived with Yeats as his secretary in Sussex, and having been Joyce's persistent benefactor, would have the answer I sought: which was that to the best of his knowledge those things had indeed been said and that in his (Pound's) opinion Joyce had had the right idea! For the rest, my sallies got fairly short shrift. He made it clear that I overestimated Wells. And plainly he didn't think much of Shaw. Only my old hero-worship of Hudson evoked his "Evoe, Hudson!"

If, then, it wasn't exactly literature, what was it that kept the correspondence going?

Pound was a lonely man, getting along in years, who needed somebody to talk to who wasn't a fellow inmate. He started right out rapping me for talking about "imposing" on him: "You misuse the verb 'impose', failing fully to grasp that the incarcerated live largely on their post bag." I realize now that as an isolated poet Ezra needed to hear a variety of living voices, idioms, accents. A principal trait was his itch to put all his correspondents in touch with one another. He actually "ordered" a young G.I. who idolized him to come to San Diego to study under me. This should clear up the otherwise obscure references to "young Stephens." I don't think he ever quite forgave me for not following up his injunction to open a correspondence with a certain British parson, Rev. Swabey, in England, whom he loved because he credited him with the same economic beliefs as himself! But there were at least half a dozen others. To correspond with all of them would have left me no time.

Pound was constantly trying to draw me into his own perfervid antagonism to our entire "usurious" system. His special bile, I remember, was reserved for the Federal Reserve, and his favorite whipping boy was, as always, Jews, or "Kikes." (This last obsession would contribute to such conglomerates as "Kikenhower.") When I sent him a snapshot of my family, there came by return mail his felicitations: they did not visibly come from Tel Aviv. According to Ginsberg, this "suburban prejudice" was revealed to have been cured in Pound before he died. Anyway, I must have been a disappointment to him in all this; for not only was I always a perfect idiot about everything remotely connected with "Econ.," but I was also decidedly pro-Semitic, i.e., I had not grasped what a danger to the world there was in the more fanatical and organized wing of American Zionism — counterpart, it seemed, of the chauvinism of the Herrenvolk. In one of my letters I launched a set protest. But it only made things worse.

I think Pound was more interested in religion than he or his disciples have been happy to admit. I myself had been trained for the ministry at Oxford. In an early (missing) letter, I told him about my uncle Frank — a saintly man of great charm and enormous laugh — and how I, as a boy, had plucked up the nerve to ask him how with his heretical views he had contrived to retain his pastorate. He gave me a startled look and answered, with the famous laugh, "Well, you see, first I win their affection; then I undermine their faith." This story didn't go over with Pound, who put the shrewd, well-deserved question: "What faith did he undermine?" At the time of our correspondence, I was a sort of Taoist, he being, of course, a staunch Confucian. Had I only studied his Unwobbling Pivot and Confucian Odes, it is probable that we could have done much better. He was extraordinarily quick; it didn't take him long to discover the sort of renegade parson I was.

If I turn the question around and ask what sustained my own interest in the correspondence, I would have to say that it was not because of a special homage for his genius, though I was probably not above faking it a bit. He was proud, insulted, injured. I think what I admired was his character, and the crusty wit camouflaging an exceptionally capacious heart, and his high standards of conduct. Someone was right who observed what a "great American" he was. "What do they know of England who only England know?" Contrariwise, there may have been something about Pound's Americanism that I was able to glimpse more clearly than most Americans could. I liked getting his letters. If I were to do it all again, I would do much better I hope. Certainly I wouldn't let it end as it did.

The end was very sad. It came about because of some shenanigans by a friend and ex-student of mine, long dropped from sight, the one Pound refers to as the "Payne in the —?" So I have to explain about Payne. He was a young man, in very poor health and, like me, an unsuccessful poet, but more ambitious. He longed for a bit of recognition and thought he had found the way to it when he purchased, with about his last dollar, a huge old printing press. With this he published two issues of a magazine called **THE LIGHT YEAR**. In it he published two letters from Pound which I had made the mistake of showing him. Then he sent the issue to Pound, together with a copy of a long poem which I had just had privately printed called *An Oxford Odyssey*. I never read his covering letter to Ezra; I believe though that he not only informed that maker of reputations that he had not been given the priceless opportunity to notice my obscure talent, but also took the opportunity to deliver an attack on Pound for selling his work for money! The perennially impoverished poet to whom this communication was addressed was, to put it mildly, displeased.

Pound ignored Miles, but wrote to me at once. Why he, in the circumstances, was generous enough to call my poem "manifestly intelligent" I shall not know. And certainly he had the right to ask why I hadn't sent the verse directly to him — which I had no intention of doing. In the second (and last) issue of **THE LIGHT YEAR**, Miles, who had in the meantime gotten into a correspondence with a female admirer of Pound's, printed a letter from her in which she compared the poet's prowess in bed to, I think, an eagle.

I've had to insert this tasteless morsel in order to make clear why I never wrote to Pound again. He needn't, after that, have written to me. But he did once, eight months later: the letter of a very tired old man, from Brunnenburg Castle, Tirolo. I was a fool to let that one go unanswered. But I did. I was so crushed by what had happened, and behind my back, that I could think of nothing but slipping as unobtrusively as possible into the silence which also enveloped him. True, the original point of writing to him had gone. I had wanted, once, to enliven a few minutes of his St. Elizabeths days.

Yet I did write to him again — a postcard from Simla, in the U.P., close to where I was born. I wanted to tell him that he was right and I was wrong about something. But this was eleven years later. I am not sure that I addressed the card right. In any case, it is doubtful that he would have remembered me.

JOHN THEOBALD

Introduction

COMIC, POIGNANT AND PAINFUL by turns, these letters illustrate, sometimes in a disarmingly genial way, one of the grimmer and more ironic episodes of modern literary history—ironic not only in that Ezra Pound should have been imprisoned in a madhouse at all, but also in that the poet of Confucian measure and discipline should have descended to raging. Here we see the "caged panther" striking out in his wrath. Yet these bitter notes are drowned out by an underlying optimism, a faith in possibilities that was always one of Pound's most engaging characteristics. The letters are full of an irrepressible, almost religious, conviction about a sound system of education for America, based on the "classics," that would bring general enlightenment and clear up the contradictions of an entire culture.

These letters make fascinating ideograms of the poet's state of mind in 1957, when his imprisonment had dragged on for over ten years with hope for release alternately glimmering and receding, while work on the later *Cantos* drew toward a kind of climax. Eagerly seizing up John Theobald as a potential convert, Pound sets about instructing him in his program, engaging all kinds of thorny issues. All his life controversy had excited him; and he seems to have found (as Joyce's Stephen Dedalus remarks, ironically, of Jews) storm to be a shelter.

There are many bristling issues in these letters besides Pound's (profoundly regrettable) anti-Semitism—his contempt for public education ("God damn it, when they offer William instead of Henry [James], and Shapiro before Eliot, and Faulkner before old Ford, it is time to look to the stalls in Augean garage . . ."), his suspicion of a "conspiracy" to do away with the study of the classics and to promote bureaucratic "crushing of ALL local civilizations in favour of uniformity and central tyranny," and so on—but most certainly, anti-Semitism is the most spiny and problematical.

Pound was drawn into the turmoil about Jews and war and money and land in the disorienting time of the first World War, which he spent in England. In 1914, like many, he took the war somewhat lightly at first, quoting in a letter to Harriet Monroe the *mot* of a friend that it was too bad that both sides couldn't be beaten. He categorized the conflict as one between both German "atavism" and the lazy corruptness of the democracies, "the loathsome spirit of mediocrity cloaked in graft," and questioned whether "the war is only a stop-gap. Only a symptom of the real disease."

As the war went on, and the casualties mounted into the millions, with each side sacrificing lives wholesale for the possession of what seemed but a few yards of mud, such levities were quickly forgotten. The combination of stalemate and slaughter maddened and terrified Pound, much as it did the average European; but also he felt peculiarly vulnerable and guilty and exposed, as an American living in England at a time when it began to seem clear that only American intervention was likely to put an end to the horror. Pound's tone in his comments about America became very bitter, sometimes hysterically so. He attacked President Wilson and the whole nation for continued neutrality. The "last public act of Henry James," that of becoming a British citizen in 1916, moved Pound deeply; and it inflamed him all the more that America, predictably, paid little notice. When America did enter the war, and it ended, Pound was one of the many to make a resolve that it must never happen again. But because of the particular psychic pain he had suffered in witnessing the spectacle, that resolve became a mania about ferreting out the war's causes; he seems to have felt much more obsessive about this than Americans who fought in the war, and a fortiori more than those who had stayed home. So he set out on a kind of crusade to probe the aetiology of war. For the student of the Cantos, certain parallels instantly spring to mind: Odysseus, at the end of the war against Troy, picking his way back through delays and disasters to Ithaca; Pound at the end of World War I picking his way through the rubble that had been European civilization, in quest of origins, causes, roots. It was just at this time that he was introduced to the economic ideas of C.H. Douglas, an iconoclast who believed that inherent defects existed in the distribution system of capitalism (though not in the production system) which made inevitable both poverty and recurrent wars.[1] Finally and fatefully Pound came to side with those who thought they perceived a conspiracy between the "merchants of death," or munitions makers, and some vaguely defined gang of "international financiers." The grudges of Western culture against Jews came to inhabit that vagueness.

The need to search out the cause of such a murderous and pointless war obsessed many besides Pound. The "merchants of death" charges were taken seriously enough to warrant Congressional investigations, unfortunately inconclusive. But Pound now saw his villain in the money system, in what he called the "bank racket."[2] It was usura, which to

Pound meant far more than excessive interest-taking, that had rotted European culture, producing not only endemic wars but also crass commercialization of all values: social, intellectual, artistic. This conviction was just close enough to certain current sterotypical accusations against Jewish moneylenders to provide a loose fit; and foreseeably the distinctions were blurred, gradually, both by Pound and by those who disputed with him. For many years, at least since "How to Read" (1929), Pound had held that poets were stewards of a culture's political health and morale. In the *Cantos* and his letters Pound talks about the rot of commercialization among Stuart Englishmen and Renaissance Venetians, and his animus against "Presbyterian bankers" and slum-lords (see *Canto* XII) was quite ecumenical. But eventually the shadowy image of the vile financiers assumed a Jewish cast.

Pound put the blame on an age-long conspiracy dominated by rich cosmopolitan Jews such as the Rothschilds. He even went so far as to believe that they had infiltrated not only Western economic institutions but also its intellectual ones, such as the Church (a theme that recurs often in these letters) in order to conceal the conspiracy. But this was not a standard brand of anti-Semitism; Pound did not begin with a prejudice against Jews which he then buttressed with economic "evidence." In fact, though in the frenzied period of World War II he accused Jews of centuries of conspiracy, it was definitely not his habit to denigrate the ordinary middle-class or shopkeeper Jew. As late as 1937, in *Guide to Kulchur,* Pound could still write that "race prejudice" was a "red herring." Only in the manic later St. Elizabeths years, but even then by no means consistently, did he drop the distinction in favor of personal ventings of frustration, thus betraying his own principle of seeking always for "gradations and discriminations."

As for the vulgarity with which he voiced his opinions, Pound had long since adopted a pose, years before race or economics entered the picture, to "save the public's soul by punching its face." This was his motto in the Vorticist period (1914-15), when he and Wyndham Lewis had put out the journal **BLAST**—the title to be construed as an imperative, or execration. "CURSE abysmal inexcusable middle-class," says **BLAST**, "(also Aristocracy and proletariat)." A perusal of Pound's Vorticist writings will reveal his constant insistence on being as offensive as possible in making statements designed to get before the public: "To the present condition of things we have nothing to say but *merde,* and the wild new scuplture says it." And so on. Having sworn eternal vigilance against politeness in public matters, Pound took every opportunity to exploit touches of vulgarity, usually with entertaining, sometimes tiresome, results. Even his beloved Italy is often "Woptalia" in his letters.

Pound chose a rhetorical pugnacity, egged on by friends like Yeats, who thought more artists had been ruined by wives and children than by dissoluteness, and who gave Pound "considerable encouragement to tell people to go to hell, and to maintain absolute intransigence." So Pound kept gentility for his private life, and turned his public face against repectability—"Salute [it] with your thumbs at your noses." [It is instructive to compare the often graceful tone of Pound's letters to his close friends with these spiky letters to Theobald, very much a member of "the public." The anti-Jewish remarks and many others should be seen as part of this habit of calculated offensiveness, a habit that became a vice (that "stupid suburban prejudice," as he later remarked to Allen Ginsberg). If you punch the public face too often you may find you're entangled with a Tar Baby.]

As the vituperative attacks on Jews, money magnates, "commies" and the like make clear, the frantic denunciatory mood of the wartime radio broadcasts was still strong in him, and imprisonment only strengthened his self-righteousness. His insistence that he had all the evidence needed to prove the existence of a conspiracy by Jews and usurers to undermine the Western world looms large and ugly in these letters; still worse, it is often expressed in petty and vulgar phrasing that makes the great poet, friend of Yeats and Eliot and Williams and Henry James, sound like a McCarthyite crank. However, although it does not excuse the deplorable character of the beliefs involved, the vulgarisms are a deceptive appearance, part of Pound's cagey mask for facing the world. And these unpleasant moments in the letters, when Pound arrogantly demands that everything be seen his way, are lightened by the curiously selfless nature of his protestations: mistaken though his principles may have been, one must admire his willingness to suffer ill-treatment for them without excessive complaint.

The approach of war had agitated Pound's worst fears, and made him frantic: all that he had set out to do seemed worse than useless, as the implacable money forces pushed the nations to the brink of their own destructions. As Pound saw it, Roosevelt and Churchill conspired to bring America into the war. True to his beliefs, Pound cherished the illusion that he could talk the United States out of the war. [In the letters to Theobald, all this still rankles. If he hadn't been right, why was he treated as dangerous?]

For making the Rome broadcasts, Pound was remanded, presumably for the rest of his life, to a federal institution for the criminally insane in Washington, D.C., where during a dozen years the present letters, among many others, as well as several books, were written. In Pound's own opinion, given in *The European*, August 1958: "Misprision of Treason [is] what I *would* have been guilty of had I not" made the broadcasts.[3] Making them came close to costing him his life.

The major events of his life from the time of the initial arrest and imprisonment to his release in 1958 are familiar: capture by partisans, and fear of execution; prolonged exposure in an iron cage at the brutal Disciplinary Training Center at Pisa, producing real collapse; the aborted trial, and the barbarity of the first year at St. Elizabeths, in the solitary ward or "hell hole" ("Problem now is not to go stark screaming hysteric"); only after this the access to the lawn, to an increasing flow of visitors and to a real opportunity to write and translate. Then came fortune's buffets and rewards: the Bollingen Prize for Poetry in 1948 was followed by rending and acrimonious controversy, and so on. It was a gruesome but epic episode in the history of American letters, and unsurprisingly produced the mixed state of mind we see in these letters.

The wonder is that Pound wasn't crushed in the process, or silenced, at least. Not that he escaped unharmed, for he didn't: "Don't expect too much—the top level of my mind is gone" (to Donald Pearce, 1952); "I cannot make it cohere" (*Canto* CXVI); the unfathomable silence of the last years in Italy. But he had always been extraordinarily resilient.

The style of his letters is springy, elliptical, increasingly telegraphic: this doesn't signify impatience on Pound's part, or annoyance with a disturber of the peace. Quite the contrary. He manifestly enjoyed writing letters, as long as he could detect some intelligence in the correspondent and the presence of a problem reasonably within his range—in John Theobald's case, an idea for a poetry anthology in which living poets would be represented by poems of their choosing, a notion that struck Pound as having some obvious merit. And so the present correspondence began.

For the student of Pound as a poet and as a maker of poetic history, the major interest of these letters is their relation, often stunningly direct, to the *Cantos*. Coke, Blackstone, and Magna Charta; Anselm, Herbert of Cherbury, and Rémusat; Kung, Linnaeus, and Agassiz; Rock, Goullart, and the Na Khi: these sets of names and ideas figure similarly in both texts, and it should become clear, as Pound's attempts to turn Theobald from a mere well-wisher into an enlightened convert suggest, just how intensely didactic those late *Cantos* were intended to be. In the letters, the complexity and esoteric nature of Pound's lessons left Theobald all at sea again and again, and when faced with incomprehension Pound usually moved off at a tangent. But the opaque phrases and obscure references in the letters were usually clarified in the course of time. Somewhat like a Zen master, Pound preferred the oblique and laconic to the directly explanatory, and often frustrated poor Theobald just as he does many readers of the *Cantos*. So the letters are like the poetry in a number of ways, even typographically. And though it is patently absurd to blur all differences and ignore all dissimilarities between the conventions of a *Canto* and those of a letter, it must be recognized that all of Pound's writing (and speaking too) is of a piece, and forms a continuum. These letters offer several kinds of instructive comparisons to Pound's poems.

Lacking space here for a full analysis of what the figures mentioned meant to Pound, at best a few simplified principles can be touched upon. His citation of the English constitutional tradition from Magna Carta to Blackstone is revealing of Pound's basically libertarian (*not authoritarian*) politics, as well as of his interest in his own legal rights; even more important, it displays his faith in documents as cornerstones of culture. In his view, certain textual traditions build up to high points at which they manifest bright and blinding truths; thus man through writing approaches the empyrean. Pound was never more American than in his reverence for constitutions, and his focus on texts bears also on his own aims and ambitions for poetry: the *Cantos* are meant to function as dynamic-display cases for such intertextual relationships. Another facet of Pound's poetics was his veneration of exact definition, precise demarcation, "luminous detail": for these Kung (Confucius), Linnaeus, and Agassiz stand—recall especially the anecdote of "Agassiz and the fish" in the *ABC of Reading*. What unifies these poetic principles, of course, is Pound's unbounded faith in the efficacy of proper procedures of exposure. He always believed that the most complicated issues could be effectively penetrated by those who would read a selected series of texts: hence his canon of authors in "How to Read" and the *ABC of Reading*, the "Square Dollar" series, the Pound-Spann anthology (*Confucius to Cummings*) that was apparently prompted by Theobald's aborted one, and the *Cantos* themselves. In fact Pound's lifelong mission was to run an intellectual chain-letter, so to speak; he was sure that if Theobald would read the required texts and communicate with other potential disciples living in California, he could start a ripple effect of some force—and the *Cantos* were meant to cause similar tides. In St. Elizabeths, as it happens, Pound did start a chain letter: eight or ten participants were sent cryptic one-liners, such as "Alexander paid the debts of his soldiery," or "Nation silly to borrow its own," and were asked to comment, then send it along to the next link. The process broke down after a few rounds, much to Pound's annoyance.

Both letters and poems failed to achieve this kind of objective, of course, and for much the same reason. The lapidary concision that is the mark of Pound's great poetry also made him a relatively ineffective expositor, especially of other men's views. Though there was in his makeup a strong streak of the teacher, the preacher, the "village explainer" (Gertrude Stein's phrase), Pound at his best was laconic, oblique, intensely concentrated: he embraced the motto *"dichten= condensare,"* found by Basil Bunting in a German-Italian dictionary. He curbed his tendencies toward garrulous expansiveness by practicing the *haiku*, the epigram, the *sottisier* or collage of dryly presented quotations from newspapers and other sources of obtuseness. In the *Cantos*, the techniques of condensation led to breathtaking lyric phrases, but also prevented explanations of opaque quotations, unclear references, and the like. Bunting accused Pound of alluding too much and presenting too little, which can be the result of over-condensation. Pound's communicatory nature was often at war with itself: to reveal or to conceal?

T.S. Eliot had earlier remarked that Pound's intense desire for his readers to know all about, say, Martin Van Buren, sometimes overwhelmed and silenced his willingness to inform them about him. There are times when he simply will not tell: *tempus loquendi, tempus tacendi.* In the letters to Theobald, Pound acknowledges his wife's complaint: "My longsuffering consort sez I so OFTEN leave out the POINT."

Lending a hand had been a lifelong habit of Pound's. "The strange thing is that Ezra was so inexpressibly kind to anyone who he felt had the faintest spark of submerged talent," recalled H.D.[4] of the early years, putting her finger on the efficient cause of much of his activity from then on—a seemingly irrepressible, often frustrated, Confucian urge to respond to a fellow creature's need. A pattern of such action emerges: rescuing a stranded showgirl in Crawfordsville, Indiana; Imagism, Vorticism; glowing reviews of then-unknown writers such as Robert Frost, and D.H. Lawrence; the "Bel Esprit" project to subsidize Eliot; feeding stray cats in Rapallo; the "Ezuversity" of both the Rapallo and St.

Elizabeths years; all that correspondence with all those people who had questions that stirred his interest—which includes the present letters, among hundreds, perhaps thousands, of others. There were, of course, other motives for correspondence. Pound himself supplies the major one: "You misuse the verb 'impose'," he fires back at an apologetic Theobald, "failing fully to grasp that the incarcerated live largely on their post bag" (21 May/57). This would be doubly, indeed desperately, true in the case of an artist whose task was to "render his own time in the terms of his own time" (Ford Madox Ford) but who in fact was shut off from his time by iron bars and red brick walls. Staying alive as poet was a real issue, and it meant contact, correspondence, with live people outside the walls.

Pound had always needed an active civilization around him. When it happened not to be there, as was the case in Georgian London, Rapallo, St. Elizabeths Hospital, he inevitably began generating one by churning about, as fish do in a stagnant tank. To some extent, the present correspondence, as well as many of his activities on behalf of sundry "little mags," such as *Edge*, or *Four Pages*, should be seen as oxygenation. He depended upon an energetic and prolific context. Always, he took off from things going on in front of his eyes rather than at a distance, or off in the future; and it seems likely that Theobald's running concern with the matter of a poetry anthology may have served as a catalyst for the Pound/ Spann anthology, *Confucius to Commings*, begun, at first with repugnance, during those very months. The letters would seem to indicate as much:

> I am ready to examine text books, but damn if I read the amateur buzzards on your list (16 May, 1957)

> May be I must dive into this aquarium/cert/full of contagions. How far you got wiff your text bk? I sure wanna see that one as soon as? (3 Sept.)

> I wd/like . . . to know what ten poems J.T. thinks no freshman shd/be without. I am KOlecting . . . (11 Sept.)

> And the Junior Anth/ is 186 pages or under 6000 lines, so there will be VERY few tax-paying-at-present writers in company with Homer, Cavalcanti etc. . . . It aint a slumming expedition . . . (17 Sept.)

Discharging his interest in Theobald's poetry anthology (which seems not to have gotten off the ground) had finally meant doing one of his own. This was, of course, thoroughly in line with his lifelong "teacher's mission." Educating, excoriating, haranguing people on a variety of public themes and issues were all facets of that mission: " . . . [I] feel that it is my job to keep a few people's attention directed toward IMMEDIATE needs." When a civilization is headed for disaster it is perfectly normal for a prophetic intelligence to express itself in exasperated, even manic tones. Nudging correspondents into actual contact with each other by letter or by personal visitation was another facet: "must pool our knowledge if we mean to preserve ANY traces of civilization" (28 May/57). His firm faith in the ability of a few serious-minded individuals, working and thinking together, to enlighten themselves and so gradually to alter the flow of events, is in fact deeply and authentically American.

As Pound letters dating from this period go, these to John Theobald are on the whole fairly straightforward, though his hatred of repetition and fondness for deflection often turn sentences into semi-riddles to be deciphered by the recipient. Early in the exchange Theobald admitted to difficulties with some of them and Pound obligingly tempered the blast to the shorn lamb. There is the usual sprinkling of playful barbarisms, "Waller toot" for "Voilà tout"; some familiar caustic puns and coinages, "Stewdenks," "Libury," "Murka"; and so on. His favorite manner (appearing about 1940, though it links back to the programmatic vulgarity of Vorticism and after) is that of backwoods semi-literate—a strangely paradoxical mask, one might think, for someone as steeped in the world's great literature as Pound was, though often productive of bizarre touches of comedy when the subject under discussion is, say, Henry James: "H.J. got round to MENEY before he croaked," he writes to Theobald. "If he hadn't had bright's disease, herman's disease, bullowayo's disease, etc., I might have got MORE into his nutt." But the one impression Pound refused to give was that of a polished man of letters—an Edmund Gosse, let us say, or indeed, the "reverend Eliot." Real insider, he deliberately chose to come on as rude outsider. Such ironic self-deprecation is not without precedent. Socrates liked to play the somewhat similar game of naive country boy in the big city. Nearer home, there are such Poundian prototypes as Bertran de Born, Peire Vidal, and François Villon, all of them accomplished literary technicians posing as anti-literates. And one recalls the later Yeats' fondness for the masks of beggarman, fool, wild old wicked man, crazy Jane. Pound's idiom was an ironic way of presenting his strident didacticism. Defending the prosaic, treatise-like vein in certain stretches of the Cantos, in one letter (20 Sept./59) he admonishes Theobald: "Am merely fighting the bunshoppe and artyshoppe boys/re/Right of bard to mention serious subject. Whether he can ketch the Konscience of the kink or merely poke Polonius in the gibblets." Certainly one of the most important services of Pound's Cantos, indeed of his whole career, was his effort to extricate from poetry and poetics the diluted aestheticism—the "taste for the unreal"—that had been the inheritance of his generation.

Difficulties of interpretation in Pound's letters usually have to do with "laconism," as he himself terms it, rather than obscurity of thought or reference; with omission of transitions between ideas (notebook fashion— the principle of the ideogram) rather than incoherence in the ideas themselves. He always hated waste motion and refused to belabor the obvious. In this, as in so much else, his acknowledged master was Confucius: "One should eliminate words that do not function." Ellipsis is an act of moral choice. The present letters sometimes admittedly make difficult reading, at least at first. But with a little familiarity, initial difficulties (seeming randomness, stripped syntax, etc.) largely disappear, or come to seem natural. As with the Cantos, constellations of names and allusions soon start recurring, like ideograms, or musical chords, Coke, Benton, Kung, Linnaeus, Blackstone, Zielinski, and others—men who were trying hard to get something done, often against enormous odds, something clearly defined, or driven firmly into place. The "cracker-barrel" English he liked to employ both in his letters and his radio talks was in fact a deliberate strategy. "Nothing solemn or formal will hold the American auditor," he said about the broadcasts at the time. "If I don't sound a bit cracked and disjointed, they will merely twirl the button and listen to the next comic song, dance, or ballyhoolah 'Soapopry'. " (Agenda, Spring 1979/80, p. 164.) The root of the village illiteracies in the letters is no doubt an indigenous distrust of rhetoric and eloquence, a preference for calling spades "spades," striking nails on heads; it is gestural, Pound reaching back across the centuries to the plain-speaking men and women who built the Republic in the first place, and in whose continuing existence he never ceased to believe. Which is one reason why the reading of almost any letter by Pound is such an energizing experience.

If in these letters we often see Pound with his teeth bared, underneath the fury we see something far more important: the conviction that the confusions of Western life could be illumined by the clarity of the classics. Pound always stood, whatever his misconceptions, against obfuscation and mystification—his voice makes an effective contrast to those of, for example, economics professors and others who protect the status quo by darkening counsel. "Peace comes of communication. . . . The whole of great art is a struggle for communication. All things that oppose this are evil, whether they be silly scoffing or obstructive tariffs."[5] Pound, who was as severe a critic of capitalism as any Marxist ("black

death," he called the capitalist system in *Jefferson and/or Mussolini*),
eagerly sought out all sorts of debunkings of it; for him, evil in the basic
systems of the culture went with sham in education—hence his thirst for a
new didacticism and a new educational rigor that should sweep away
such paltry devices as "creative writing" courses. The classics would be
the foundation of the curriculum: the true classics, moreover, not just the
Greco-Roman smattering that mark "gentlemen" in England. Therefore
the need for a new canon.

Pound's educational reforms are too apocalyptic to consider in detail
here, but the traces of them inhering in his letters to Theobald cast all
kinds of light on his ambitions in the *Cantos*. Even the style of these letters
is reminiscent of the poem: elliptical, allusive, intent on forcing the
reader to make connections, never giving him explicit directions. Pound
believed in a Confucian dialectic: "get the meaning across" (a precept
embodied in a Chinese character that suggested to him "lead the sheep out
to pasture")—"then stop." His obedience to that last admonition has
irritated countless readers accustomed to more discursive practices. We
who are used to having everything explained for us will find the *Cantos*
very difficult; and these letters too. But the principle of dissociation that
Pound invokes is one source of his enduring interest.[6] As one component
of the ideogram of his convictions that these letters represent, his stylistic
practice is typical and vital.

As for John Theobald's part in this correspondence, given the inherent
difficulties of the role, it is fair to say that he held his end up very well,
much better than in retrospect he seemed to feel he had. Always prompt in
his replies, sincere and independent in his views (sometimes standing up
to Pound over points on which he felt disagreement), he kept the
correspondence moving in various useful directions. And fortunately, he
had the sense to keep carbons of the letters he wrote: side by side now
with Pound's to him, they enable the reader to watch with an intimacy
otherwise impossible the workings of Pound's mind in immediate
dialogue with another.

DONALD PEARCE
HERBERT SCHNEIDAU

Pound in these early letters appears in moods of fierce depression, ranting against obscurantists who keep the truth systematically hidden; but there are lighter moments: the sarcasms about America's youth-aping faddisms, for instance. Pound's withering scorn at what his friend Wyndham Lewis had denounced as "child-cult" is typical of his long-standing denunciations; he saw himself as a fighter for sane and cleansing knowledge that would preserve at least "traces of civilization" in a country which was now buried under apathy and a preference for trivia, which in turn was the result of a sabotaged educational system. As he grasped for connections, no doubt wondering if Theobald was sufficiently hostile to current orthodoxies to see the point of his thrusts, he had to dismiss such distractions as his own early work, such poems as "The Goodly Fere" ("Christ as gangster") and "The River-Merchant's Wife."

This was a recurrent mood; he often felt more or less squeamish about the pre-Cantos poems. Here the feeling was exacerbated by the urgency he felt to get his great re-education project into motion: out there in America, he assumed, there must be a network of individuals who see through the flow of "sewage" and who need to be put in touch with each other, the better to be enlightened by a select list of works (the "Square Dollar" series was a version) that manifest revelations about our culture and its self-betrayal. Regnery, the publisher, and others for whom he had great hopes were proving recalcitrant; Poetry magazine had been a major journal for modernism when Pound was its "foreign correspondent" (1912-17) but was now "backwash of dear Harriet" (Monroe), its founder. Perhaps Pound thought, a new anthology modelled in part on a great predecessor such as the Confucian Odes could do something. What shows through, however, rather depressingly, is the tendency of Pound's all-purpose conspiracy theory to gobble up everything. "Beria," or Soviet thought-control, is behind a supposed influx of Russian or Jewish psychiatrists (who "kiketrize" and suppress freedom of inquiry.) [An observation provoked perhaps by his present situation in St. Elizabeths?] These in turn connect with Jews who have for centuries infiltrated Christian theology ("St. Ambrose" is the putative authority here), and who participated in the modern educational swindle, by which Greek, Latin and solid courses were replaced by "cWeative wYting," resulting in a flood of imitated anthology pieces: "uncontrolled Kepp'n me Kepp'n." Aside from the occasional and distasteful virulence of the anti-Semitic remarks, one of the sadder aspects of this notion is the grip it had on Pound.

P1 / TLS
                                    1

                                                               26 Ap 57

"The Goodly Fere" appeared in the International Sunday School lessons
     before you were (probably ?) born.

I spose it was considered fit for the young (in period before they
     were dopes and bobby-soxers).

I am out of law in preferring adults / but where 98% of the population
is afflicted with raging infantilism, I don't spose that matters.

If you hope to have a country in 20 years time, suggest, for personal
use, chew thru Sq $ / series, as minimum.

So far Regnery never will touch anything I think grade A/.

Has Hildebrand Un.Calif, any positive program or merely 100% JUSTIFIED
objection to present sewage??

                                              Yr, Ez Pound

P2 / TLS

2

8 Maggio '57

No idea who is Hildebrand, one of <the> most prevalent organs of
degradation and brain wash, SAID he inhabits yr/ beanery and objects
to deluge of catshit in education / BUT did not make clear if
it was REALLY the cat shit that he objects to.

Sorry you object to divergence of opinion, and plug for something
that will not jolt the unfortunate victims of degeneracy in
the post Dexter-Weiss-White era of american deliquescence.

Personally prefer bro Lightfoot to Episcopals and Shehan, Maritain
and other diluters.

Libury'em at Ham Col/ said the stewdenks were being taught acquiescence.

A terd from S.Louis definitely advised ignorance, cause he wd/ jeopard
his unwashed hide if he learned any histry.

If any READING matter got past the Chicago office, my congrats.
It takes a special alerte <to> divert me from more lively perusals
to the back wash of dear Harriet,

                    but useful to have a trade
journal.

                          cordially yrs/

I mean if something got into the Sewing Circle Gazette, I would have to
be TOLD to look for it.

May be Carruth's sorrows in that ambience wd/ move yr/ Oxonian pity??

                                  E.P.

              Why not include Hemingway's
                  Neo Thomist Poem
if you are acquiescing in the Ford philosophy, Pullitzer
        standards, and Fullblight??

P3 / TLS   **3**

16 May '57

    At any rate yr/ abbreviations are as hard on the (present)
reader as some people tell me, mine are on them.

I don't recall having suggested cantos for 14 year olds/ in fact
must be indication somewhere that I write for those who HAVE
looked at the classics/

What about the Classic Anthology, defined by Confucius, partially
printed by the unspeakable Harvards/ omitting necessary apparatus
for the serious student/

Wonder if you have seen it?

Kung not interested in what a man might do IF, but in what he can do.
//

Sq $/ (with Blackstone hoped for) should be required before end/ of
freshman year/

and anyone aware of the facts, who doesn't plug for it is wronging
the young/

P.C. Das has used my Whitman verse in *oriya* translation of Whitman,
<*very pretty type face*> says he is taking me to Orissa and Bengal

Morgenthau treasury reports might lead one to estimate even the
weight of "vested interests" in Calif/

and the stink goes back 2500 years.

Trouble with my?? (our???) generation   is that they don't
talk to each other.

             Do you actually MEET Hildebrand?
Any chance of his looking at Sq $/

                    You can't STOP the swindle of
big advertising for general poison <BUT> there IS an article on bread
in American **LEGION**/& Last issue *Mercury* also approaches
necessary clarification.

              It is the positive printing of what one can
afford to print at a loss

             which gives one a toe hold/ AND
then count on time lag/

My Lit/ Essays get to *Kleinstadt* Italy with 40 years lag/

european THOUGHT takes that to git to this side LandyGoschen.

I think you cd/ find something better in the ODES, than the
River Merchant as of 1915. If what Santayana called Christ as ganster
(yes G.S. omitted the g. and that spelling is used in europe)
is too Revivalist and unepiscopalian for yr/ anthol.

For 2000 years every FIRST rate chinaman has tried to see what cd/
be added to, or taken from, the three books / and, for 1000 years, from
the four. (i.e. when they found Mencius necessary)

Krishnamurti very MUCH heard of in London 40 years ago/

> when my Confucius "Pivot" was printed in Calcutta, Chakravarty
> said

: we have not this Confucius.

> Can you try Hildebrand on: Lincoln was shot for not understanding .

what Jefferson wrote to Crawford in 1816. <vide enc>
??

Reid struggling with a buzzard bearing the antient name of Niebuhr
??grandson??

wonder WHAT yr Unc. F/ was undermining their faith IN ???

Kung, Mencius, Dante, Agassiz seem to me to have putt it in the right
place/

> also Erigena, R. St Victor, Cherbury, Rémusat.

Several familiar lables in yr/letter/ but very vague, say, as to
ubicity of Pusey house?

Swabey who did some SERIOUS study on some of TSE's dilletante
interests still a parson, (Lincolnshire)

> view that with all that mechanism

, some use shd/ be made of it.

E. P.

P4 / TLS

4

Dear Theobald

21 Maggio '57

You misuse the verb "impose," failing fully to grasp
that the incarcerated live largely on their post bag, and that
44 years after the gt/ betrayal ANY indication that any denizen
of our ex-republic uses his mind AT ALL is a comfort.

The eggheads and univs/ having fallen from the literate level
@ which Cullen Bryant thrashed a s.o.b. on Broadway from slandering
Andy Jackson, to a period of Sandbags and Kennedies evading vital
issues in vendable (via "outlets") history.

I hear the head of our most notorious theolog/ cemetray is a kike
which wd/ be perfectly in line with tradition, as vs/ St Ambrose's
protests. I have not accepted the above statement, but there is nothing in
the bastid's utterance, which I have so far seen, to cause suspicion
of its incorrectness.

He claims friendship with the egregious Eliot,
whose omission of the G.F. from Faber's collection amused me
considerably, as well as his perfectly plausible and politic reason.

I wasn't puttin' in a plea for the style of my earlier publications, merely
ragging you re/ what was considered suitable for a large public
by a theolog/ organization nigh onto ½ a century ago.

By now you will have had suggestion for something writ with equal
clarity, at much later date.

Last week two chaRRRming young people showed signs of getting
off the Cathay mode/

my own view: that after 1915 NOBODY translated
from Chinese, but utilized an idiom, regardless of the difference
between one chinese author and another. (AND it still goes on.)

Talking of Kung with afro american on this ward, it occurs to me
that China WITH Kung has, for 2500 years, had no religious wars /
only the three jewish religions instigating the *jehads* or
contriving them.

Did you ever look into Robert's hocking of Normandy to his
Rooseveltian brother Rufus???

I am continually on the hunt for curiosity re/ various subjects
and historic characters, such as Thiers or Louis X of France,
          deploring the lack of communication between literates
in (? our) unfortunate country.

Pusey House (? London ?)

Santayana's comment

                    occurred when he told me he was writin 'bout
xt/ and I <said> what a funny subject to be doing then (1940s
instead of 1908).

                                        cordially yrs

How much of Chap II, or III of the enc/ do you spose Sandbag wd/understand?

                                                    Ez. P.

T1   **5**

1390 Merritt Dr.
El Cajon, Calif.

Dear Mr. Pound,   *May 24, 1957*

"Imposing" as I used it was without doubt an "out" for another sort of imposition, which I am in no mind to weezle about: the rank pretense of adequacy to yr allusions. I am a historic historical ignoramus, read now hardly anything (outside interminable student themes, some of them better than the pros) but certain poets and certain scriptures & commentaries, esp. the 18 principal *Upanishads* & Samkara (whose *Ode to the South Facing Form* alone says more to me than the *Phaedrus* & *Protagoras* & *Nicho. Ethics* together). I get the scholarship thro' Radhakrishnan, who from what I hear of his activities as Vice President of India, is our nearest approach to Aurelius or Julian, tho' I can't yet figure his relations with his boss, the infamous Nehru. I'm still hoping to shake off enough *acedia* to get the Sanscrit, the very sound of which gives me small memory shocks, having been born at Nina Tal in the U.P. Krishnamurti, my admiration of whom I have already conveyed to you in a hyperbolic manner, reads, as I am to understand, literally nothing at all. I knew that he broke from Earl del Warr & Annie Besant as long ago as you say, and that there was some talk then of his polite disclaimers of messianic roles. After all, Pound is not exactly unknown (tho' I own I was a little startled to get my *Spectator*—I don't order it: it is sent—yesterday and see big headlines about Pound, to find it was an Admiral that Alanbrooke is saying fouled up the naval strategy!) But the point was that you and K wd resemble each other in regard to how much you are actually read.

My Uncle Frank's heresies were for the most part, of course, christological, much harder to get away with then than fornication with choir girls. He was what I wd take to be a saintly man, but that wdn't help either. It was his personal glamour that gave him room to move about.

Pusey House. Why the hell wd I expect you to know about that? The official stronghold of the Oxf. anglocatholics and guardian of the Newman tradition—held in force on Sunday afternoons by smooth priests who wd always use the Augustine gag: "You seek to understand in order that you may believe: we believe in order that we may understand." As I indicated, they worked me over for a while (I was the boy preacher and considered a catch if I may be so vulgar as to mention it) but soon gave up.

Neither I nor my colleagues got your allusion to H'way's "neo-Thomist poem." One said he thought you must be referring to *Old Man & the Sea* but I cdn't see it. . . .

Yrs has cryptic things for me, with this fast allusary shorthand of yrs: didn't get the 2 "charrrming young people off the Cathay mode." Don't remember Santayana's comment—you didn't mean the one about "no God & Mary being his Mother"?

Didn't get about the Jewish Principal or what wd be bad about this unless, as often happens, he was also an sob. Is this Regnery? His officers are Jewish and I know he plays footsy with the RCs. Don't know St Ambrose's protests, tho' I did name one of the villains of my "Odyssey" after that hierarch. Did get the general idea that you feel no overwhelming personal affection for Mr. Eliot, and this is not going to create a strain, but Eliot is not the only celebrated poet that I could not like when I met him. In fact, it's got where I run for cover when I see them coming . . .

If you just don't count on me to know a damn thing, I can conceive a sporadic correspondence, profitable on one side only, and that not the prisoner.

> This is quite sincerely,
> John Theobald

P5 / TLS

6

J.T.

28 Maggio '57

As the vebbl/ Hem's poEM is brief, and as was error in original (sfar as known only) printing I will give it you.

NEO-THOMIST POEM

The Lord is my shepherd
I shall not want
Him for long.

Affection for Eliot about all that is left in view of what appears to me atrophy of curiosity on his part, and an unwillingness to
face specific historic facts
, necessary as I see it, to intelligence of
reality.

Only man in England who does appear to think is Swabey, whose "Church of England and Usury" is still unprinted. He went on and investigated Launcelot Andrews and translated one treatise.

Pusey, as I suspected / and damn Augustine. Bach and Tielmann much better for the mind.

Chakravarty said: India is in the hands of the industrialists, any one who opposes them will simply disappear.

Praps that's why one hears so little of Radhakrishnan.

Chak/ also said: "he is not the old Nehru." He <Chak> got the *Pivot* printed in Calcutta, from which the Sq $/ is offset. BUT they had been polite to him in Moscow.

Somewhere near you Carsun Chang has an unpublished history of neo-Confucianism/
I.e. when they pulled up their socks to reply to
hindoo invasion/
Dante "*compagnevole animale*" / Lack of adult conversation in Baruchistan very wearing. I have quoted or
at least shown awareness to Chang in later *Cantos*.

Orage drug me thru 1½ vols of *Mahabharatt* and then I stuck.

no use for Shaw.

The *Point*, 12 Bow St. Cambridge 38, Mass. quotes Ambrose, and
APO has reprinted something the bigots rather wish he hadn't
writ, if he did, and if so, it was before he was brainwashed.

No one knows enough, soon enough. Must pool our knowledge if we mean to
preserve ANY traces of civilization.

Have you any lines on Louis X, *le hutin*, of France?

cordially yrs

Ez. P.

P6 / TLS   **7**

J.T.   *29 Maggio/* just runnin' on

Of curse Eliot never
went on with his Sanskrit or with much of anything
ELSE.
yu must be ?? 68 or my age? The Blavatskites did NOT greatly
esteem ma Besant /

        G.R.S. Mead, Quest Society? ring any bells for J.T.?
serious chinks take sanskrit seriously / possibly their necessary
greek / <*possibly superior? but I am an ass re/ funny alPHabets*
Pse•los refinements. not again until Hen. James.>

       I still doubt gt/ need IF a man has grasped Confucian *metaphysika*
(usually supposed to not be).
Swabey just sent good page re/ Aristotle's mechanization vs/
Plato / <*will be in Edge*>
F. Masai, done good bk/ *Gemisto Pléthon et le Platonisme de Mistra*
        soc. G. Budé, 95 bd Raspail, Paris.
        <*last stronghold of civilization in Frogland*>
Rock on Na Khi/and lively *Forgotten Kingdom* by Goullart (Murray,
London).
Anything of Krishna M/ that I cd/ get at briefly?
alzo/ poor indian paper "Vigil" arrives but dont recall mention
of yr/ Radha /k
If the Moscovites mislike the subcontinental complexion they
conceal it with oily politeness / AND Chak, teaching at Howard
was kept in cage separate from his blonde danish wife /
               which causes nuances.
Anyone yet noted the hindoo depth in LaForgue?

                             Ez. P.

T2

8

1390 Merritt Dr.,
El Cajon, Calif.
June 1, 1957

Dear E.P. ("Mr." seems now to distort status)

Starting with the ego, which I have a nasty feeling interests me more than it does you—no: I was born Sept. 5, 1903, and I *ought* to have conveyed the attitude of a junior, I mean aside from yr fame. I mean otherwise I have been fresh.

Krishnamurti's strong suit is standing under an oak and answering questions in an entirely forthright manner, without any apparent narcissism, such as the usual attempts at whimsy, etc., etc. Most of his books are tape recordings of these performances in India, California, Holland, England, and elsewhere. However, as I think I mentioned, *Harper* recently (1956) came out with the first book he actually *wrote*, called *Commentaries on Living*. It is $3.50. If you don't have access to a library, I shd feel privileged to lend you my copy. He is a trifle proud for some tastes, but there are evidences that he is sick of sycophants as well as obscurantists and other varieties of knaves and fools. I have heard him hold forth but did not introduce myself. Too many people pawing him. In India they don't go out of their way to shake hands. Rhadakrishnan's mighty tome, as you probably know, is also Harper: *The Principal Upanishads*, with perfectly magnificent apparatus (1953). I don't think he had gone to Moscow then, so he must have done it at Oxford. Don't see how he stood it there. . . . Incidently, while on books, how is Ben Nelson's (Columbia) *Usury in the Middle Ages*?

Please take back my sniping at Eliot: out of place: something about the urbanity that always made me fidgety. You can't pick a fight about Shaw, except I get a charge out of some of the clowning in the prefaces, and the watered down Nietzsche may have helped in its day—N himself not being around to see it through. I did do a doctoral dissertation on D.H. Lawrence which leaned rather heavily on *Birth of Tragedy*, but looking at it now is not a very happy experience. L not only disappointed about God and sex, but if I am to believe what Aldous H. tells me, was a disappointed painter at the end. I saw a couple of his canvases at Taos before Frieda died. Not bad.

Nobody around here seems to know anything about Louis X. What precisely do you refer to as "the great betrayal"?

Ashamed to say I never read La Forgue tho' my previous friend J.C. Powys compared my *New Venus & Adonis* to that—suspect because JCP didn't know much about verse.

Was Mead one of the Psychical Research investigators that made trouble for Blavatsky? I connect him vaguely with Kingsland & the neo-Blavatskikes (no Pound pun intended). I never could figure out quite about the *Secret Doctrine*; can't help admiring Ernest Wood's "Digest," but then Wood's a fine fellow.

Can't really answer your highly charged epistolary telegraphs, but here's to you with another laborious footnote.

J.T.

After a time the letters begin to reveal more spiritual interests. Pound's fascination with the rites of the Na Khi tribe of western China will appear in Cantos 98 and 104, and his interest in Richard of St. Victor and Herbert of Cherbury in Cantos 100, 101, and 109. Pound questions Theobald about his awareness of the milieu of London in the early 1900's, when W.B. Yeats and G.R.S. Mead instructed him in theosophical and other mysteries. Here Pound's anecdotes (e.g. Madame Blavatsky as a Gertrude Stein figure), rich in themselves, mask one of the enduring interests of his life, so evident in the visionary traditions invoked in the Cantos. Though early on he had tried Yeats' spiritualism (see The Letters of Ezra Pound 1907-1941, ed. D. D. Paige [New York: New Directions, 1971], pp. 139-141), he retained all his life his own early convictions about the "truths" of mythology and ritual and augmented them with kindred materials, such as those given by Rock and Goullart.

Other names that appear here include Hugh Kenner (with whom Theobald did not appear to get along), J.C. Chatel, and David Gordon, of the St. Elizabeths circle of Pound's close associates; "Watts" is Harold Watts, though Pound forgets his first name and Theobald has Alan Watts in mind; "King Bolo" is T.S. Eliot's obscene poem, never published, sufficiently strong stuff to make Pound wary of showing it to James Joyce (Letters, p. 171). The "Bubblegum" award is of course the Bollingen. McAlmon is Robert, companion of Pound and Hemingway and others in Paris in the twenties; "Amy" is Lowell, whose corpulence as attested by photographs was even greater than Pound's jibes suggest; "Nic Smeary Butter" is Nicholas Murray Butler, another rogue in Pound's gallery, president of Columbia University and the Carnegie Endowment. For "hic est medium mundi," see Canto 87. Condé Nast, publisher, stands for "magazines in general." Eva Hesse, of course, is Pound's German translator. (Most such references, in fact, get adequately explained in the course of later letters.)

An important issue that surfaces here, however, is Pound's insistence on the political aims of the Cantos, and his comparison of his work to Dante's and to Shakespeare's Histories, in ABC of Reading called "the true English epos." Pound reiterates the point that Charles I was beheaded thirty-three years after Shakespeare's death, which inevitably implies that Shakespeare's "objection to unlimited monarchy" in the history plays helped set revolutionary events in motion. Eliot's failure (in After Strange Gods) "to understand my picture of the mind of England in Cantos XIV?XV" (see letter of July 2, 1957) was a failure, purely and simply, to perceive the relations between economic events in the public realm of the nation and those in the inner realm of the poem. "Homer, Dant, Shx," he insists, "were CONCERNED with economics." Pound had believed, at least from World War I on, that art had to be didactic (see Letters, p. 190) and that "artists are the antennae of the race."

P7 / TLS

9

3 June   Bghsz

Thank gawd fer foto of fambly with no relations in Tel Aviv
            and possibly none in the State Dept/

Some APO can probably get bks/ from library / G.G. supplying those from
Cat. Univ. Migne, etc.

Have not seen the Nelson/Swabey unpublished on Ch. of Eng. and Usury.
(pardon if I repeat, cant remember whom I tell what)

GRS Mead / BlavatskiTe (no suspicion of a k) "Echoes from the
Gnosis," possibly 40 vols/

            Quest Society and Quarterly, Q.S. lectures at least
monthly for part of year/ <London 19? to '14>.

lack of humour, vurry amusin to Yeats / also caused Eliot's
HIGHEST bit of repartee /

M/ surprised to see E.P. at meeting of Aristotelian Society
(description of scene unfamiliar to J.T.)

Possum languidly: Oh, he's not here as a phiLOSopher, he's
            here as an AnthroPologist.

No sign up, vs/ sniping at T.S.E. I have been doing it for years/
BUT . . . .

Ford groaned re/ Prufrock: You'll let back ALL the academicisms.

Powys who I met about 1910 never cd/ quite stand me/

I don't think Mead mucked with the psychical research gang/ that was
another subject of satire/
            Fielding and Miss Tomczyk etc.

yes, Shaw amusing to univ. stewdent in 1902 or thaaarbouts/

ever see foto BEFORE the whiskers?

If not consult recent TIME for phiz of Connant (NO, not same
            totem . . .butttt . . . .

I meant it was Chak/ to whom purrlightness shown in Moscow,
            know nowt re/ yr/ Rhada . . .

                    benedictions and saluti alla famiglia

There are several more items due to appear in *Edg/* the Calif. Univ. lie
BURIED will need it/ *Little Rev/* full set finally sold for
$750

Ez. P.

P.S. neX day on mediation. If you are strapped/, why not work out yr
road tax, *i.e.* EDGE -scription by doing two pages re what the *Upanishads*
have that Kung fu tseu hasn't. Am skeptical re/ its being anything
necessary, but *Edge* readers will want to know about Rhadakrishnan version.
I enc/ note of Swabey's, later revised, as an introduction to him,
you can refer to it if relevant to above, as it will have appeared
by the time yr/ note gets to Stock, or cd/ appear simult.

John Berry who is trying *epos* on hindoo lines, been several years out there
was when last heard of somewhere in Calif. in fact no reason yr/
progeny shdn't prepare to have other mental contacts than themes
suffered by *padre* in line of profession. I mean even if yr/ reclusion
is intentional/ No idea which Caltropolis is nearest El Cajon. Kenner
trying to gather less idiot jr/ profs into his beanery. in fact life of
the mind, not that K/ always knows what it is . . . Swedenborg on
"composed of societies."
for gt/ betrayal, see MULLINS on the Federal Reserve. date dec 23,
1913, Jekyl Island.

10

Dear E.P.,

June 7

My kicks re chosen people might turn out to diverge fr yours. They
certainly have no right in Tel Aviv & the way I heard it showed no interest
in that territory till they ascertained the presence of oil, etc. there; tho'
who the hell else wd take them you tell me? Their famous extortionary
proclivity has probably had better excuses than the Xians' ditto, in my
view, since Jews are tent-nomads versus cave-dwellers and there must
have been times when they couldn't be fussy to survive. If they killed their
avatar, the Xters did a more effective job of that in the end, surely. As to
their general halitosis, doesn't it lead from their weird superiority
complex, in their Fraud's jargon,—*cringed over*: and the whole reverting
to the Yahweh monopoly, in which they are again excelled by the Xians,
esp. R.C.'s, who considered as extortionists (from what I saw in Rome last
summer) wd make their rivals look like pikers. — What the hell are Jews
to do except renege their roots, and one does see some of them do a lot of
that: no easy matter when you consider they are raised stricter than
southern Pentecostals. (Incidentally Jews are seldom killers like the
southerners *et al.*) P.S. Without the Oppenheimers your sales would
surely have taken a dip . . . . Thought I ought to expose these few fragrant
platitudes to your severe gaze, partly to indulge the racial theorizing fad,
and partly not to welch on some good eggs.

What does Swabey mean by "ON not to say JAH"? Particularly liked what
he said of "envy", never far from ambition . . . .

Very nice of you to suggest that way of earning *Edge*, but I repeat, "Depart
from me . . . ." Don't have what it would take right now. I'll just buy the
mag.

Fancy you knowing JCP! Did he propitiate rocks and stones and trees? He
must always have been too eloquent — "BUT . . ." (as you say of Eliot)

Just got 2 free unpublished poems for my anthology from my favorite
British survivor, Herbert Read, knighted now, I guess. Ever know him?
Something about him. Best American letters too were from best
Americans—Pound, W.C. Williams, Cummings and now a poet called
Roethke. Stevens unfortunately gone. There'll be others here but England
seems to be dying of some sort of auto-poisoning. Powys once informed
me England the place for the very young and v. old and he was going back
to "lay down his bones" there. Can't see they have done much for him

since he left the Catskills where he wd stare at detailed maps of Glastonbury to get a new novel on the fire, then pull Dickensian names out of a hat and allow the bowels to disgorge as they would . . . .

Mead! Of course, of course! Why, I have the *Pistis Sophia* right here on my shelf. Believe I prefer his sidekick Kingsland who had the trick of picking the gnostic heart out of holy writ. Can't help feeling all those pariahs had a tooth for the truth. At least they knew that dish was neutral in gender, simple in smell, and singular, not (except in a plural sense) plural. What is E.P.'s recollection (unless it's all old hat) as to Yeats' REAL attitude to Blavatsky? No, of course it was Myers *et al* who sent the sleuth (Hodgson) to India after her, where it looks to me my Dad's colleagues (missionaries) framed her—smeared her, as the commies say . . . . Hope I don't bore you on the subject of that land. It doesn't even have to be true to enthrall me. Have just read Brunton's book (*Secret India*) with a style to set your teeth on edge. True? Not? Don't know, I eat it up. Rankest journalese and I swallow it like a pill . . . .Somebody ought to write just one perfectly beautiful book about India.

Yours,
John Theobald

P8 / TLS **11**

J.T. 11—Giugn '57

Thanks yrs/ Swabe enc'd. Yeats: Blavatsky, OBjective, as per
sitting at table digging into juicy beefsteak / disciples on carrot
diet: "Ah, chilDren, my CHILdren, how many of you have succeeded . . .
in . . . BEgetting vegeTARian children?"
Also her pulling Mead's leg to see whether M/ thinking or
swallowing.

W.B.Y. inveterate gossip, love of anecdote & hvg/ insufficiently
jecte sa gourme en jeunesse, unduly excitable over items which wd/
not move any who had cut milk teeth on Propertius and Martial / also
on spooks etc/ to the joye of Dulac, y.v.t. and the irreverent
younger Gonne's, per es/ Iseult's delight in my "Uncle William with
seven bees in seven separate bonnets."

Powys staggering, at least literarily, behind a loaded phallos
with hyper Laurentian (D.H.) zeal and empressment / met but known
more indirectly as he had married a she enthusiast to a less exhuberant
henchman, and she (a friend of H.D.'s) whom I knew fairly well during
stay in U.S. 1910. J.C. usually given as "Jhezus Christ Powys"
in familiar converse in that restricted circle.
Believe JCP regarded me a bit as you do Eliot, plus
considering me . . . not sure if THAT was JCP, but one of 'em . . .
simple but something or other.
Neither JCP nor DHL, as I saw it, in W. Lewis category.
Lawrence almost alone in seconda, as distinct from terza and quinta
categoria.

I think Mead must hv done "nigh onter" 40 vols, of Echoes, and the
Quest ¼ ly must have run at least ten years??

Must ref/ yu <to> printed re/ mesopotamia/ The Point,
12 Bow St. Cambridge 38, Mass
had a vigorous quote from Ambrose last autumn. Already in Bede's time
the clean Xters objecting to concessions to judaism/ ?? any literate
before 300 take the stuff save as SYMBOL?
vid. Zielinski for origins of dogma.
Anselm a sane trinity / also essentia being feminine, mere grammar
gives you a B.V.M.

Dante, *De Monarchia*, "more than half the job done by
Ari in *Nichomachian Etica*."

I take it Swb/ means a gk/ and a kike *deus* / On, Jah.

His apol/ that "<with> all this mechanism (*i.e.* episc.) some use ought
to be made of it." <*established ch. of Eng.*>

The Rev. Galton (Arthur) under Ancastor aegis, bequeathed his
Beaumarchais "Voltaire" in umpty vols/ to my consort or her ma,@
any rate it is part of intimate cultural heritage.

Herbie Read, know slightly, find a bit arid. Was present one p.m.
in '38, with reps/ of several brit/ activities / but I doubt if you
can get him to come clean of Gesell, or Elsom or any real history.

> Two denuntiations of Sandbag's *Lincoln*, <since I wrot you>
> in reply to enquiry.

Old Scharmel Iris *sic:* "made box office out of Honest Abe who got
shot
because of money, the money slid over in Lincolniania. Why in hell
cant he give it to us straight?"

> Chatel having looked at all refs/ to money in index
reports no honesty on the subject, and damn little mention.

> I have a 2 vol. Cavour / two passages, about ¾rs of
a page *in toto*, re/ said delicate subject.

No I didn't mean employ Berry, doubt if he wants to do anything
but contemplate / BUT bigob if you cd/ get Chao you wd/ have a treasure.
probably knows more Tu Fu than any / AND has just dug up Kuan Chung.

MOST important economist recommended by Confucio / I thought he had
been lost in burning of books / am awaiting further data from Chao.

AND metric renovation has a lot to hope from chinese metric/
which the swine at Harvard delay revealing/ though keep on murmuring
that they aint crooks, and that their contract was just their way of
putting it, and I shdn't have expected a time element to function.

Chao ought not to be wasted / more data if any chance of your getting
him <a job>.

Brunton ?? egyptologist, London 1914 ? or some other. Worked with
Petrie.

Kingsland only a name to me.

Miss Tseng's bro/ now head of Tunghai, Formosa Univ.
S/ thinks Chao cdn't go there, cause commies ready to murder his
relatives on mainland if he shows signs of favouring civilization.

        con espressioni di alta stima etc.

Magnif/ (portagoose) trans/ *Canto 20*, front page *Jornal do Brasil*.

Oriya Whitman recd. from Das

both Chao and Wang in *Edge*/ Chao 20 years older/ Wang foolishly asked
Fullblight or someone to finance a thesis in Ezrolologie,
and naturally no Univ. wd/ have him, tho Loré got 1½ years
under Kenner/ coming deepchestedly <*"Child of Vaterland" H.J.*>
front on / the fragile
A.B. from our native shores was told "*they* didn't mind, but thought
it wd/ be blocked in lower echelons." <*as it was*>

    did I quote "*confirma*" from Italy, after visit from their 2nd.
ranking versifier: USIS run by communist jews, when they cant give
scholarships to jews, they give 'em to communists or at any rate pinks
who havent even guts to be commies.

                                        Ez. P.

P9 / TLS   **12**

J.T.   *12 Giugn '57*

     several points missed in my yester reply. When yu say yu "ain got wot," I spose you mean that you dont know Kung well enough to make confronto with *Upanishads.* Can you give ME any idea what is there /
I think I said I got stuck in vol/ 2 *Mahabharata/* and used the *Kamasutra* in "Jodindranath's occupation" / an irreverence.

     Know anything of Jos Pijohan, whom Glenn Frank (whom I supposed a bit empty in some sections) roped into "University of Knowledge."
Omit the "h" Pijoan, art prof at U. of Chicago in 1940. one intelligent page in *Outline Hist. of Art.*

     Carsun Chang, address 2295 Hanover St. Palo Alto.
I sd ? Hist. neo-Confucianism, unpubd/ but you can correlate
re/ Zen. fruit of impact of India on China, and Confucian
reinvigoration <has> long past, as head of some chink univ. BUT got a lot of useless european philos. injected earlier, not permanent poison.

John Berry 317 Fifth St. Huntington Beach, Calif.
               for conversation/ he must know bengali and/or sanskrit
               <or both>
several years out there and to Santiniketan (Tagore joint) but not headed to, or centered in Tagorism.

The man for your dept is Chao (agitated telegram <this a.m.> that trans/ of Kuan Chung is not his. details later.)

Chang over 60, but I think Chao needs job worse. AND distinctly of use re/ metric, which I dont spose Chang has thought about.
Wang "the most confident y.m."/, as I think I sd/ on war path.

At least invite C.C. and JB to tea. Yes, the Swedenborg must be in "Heaven and Hell," all I had read at date @ which I started quoting that sentence.

        Santayana cd/ take interest in Spinoza, Swed/ just didn't seem to him. Also he didn't think he "wd/ like" speaking on Radio Roma. marano angle. one might suppose.

Wonder was yr Kingsland the bloke Florence Farr quoted to effect: *beato Jesu* and initiate, non-kike, punished for revealing mysteries to the prophane?

Fascist secretary Rapallo much amused by dutch jew howling that the franciscans who helped him smuggle cash into woptaly had put the bite on him for more % than . . .

queery as to whether the Blavat/ wasn't a super Gertie (Stein) dealing
in *Upanishads* rather than Picassos. and knowing, nacherly, more of
the subject than rural yokels, G.I. of ist/ war or ult/ brits
on 1900 or 1880?

        physiognomy / Eusapia Paladino etc.

Zen, plus guilds in Byzantium/ vocational representation/

        I think this manages to *aggiornare* with yrs/ 7th inst.
mebbe yu orter hv/ copy of *Current*/ <enc> re yr/ ist, paragraph/ not that
it contains any novelties. Did I ask if you want spare copy
of "Moribus Brachmanorum"? or did I send you one?

The "beautiful book" is Goullart's "Forgotten Kingdom" / Murray, 50
Albermarle St, London W. 1. last year, a bit north of yr/ *Gebiet*
but cert not to be missed.

                                    Yrs. *E.P.*

13

Dear E.P.,   *June 14, 1957*

I have two of yrs. *"I-Giugn"* (meaning *"11-Giugn"*?) and an absorbing footnote, *"12 Giugn,"* both making motions to prod me out of my 50-yr sleep. Probably hopeless as far as my own literary prospects go, but anything at all we can do to help spring you, I wd wish to be informed. Surely there must be something *unnecessarily* unavailing in the ACADEMIA BULLETINS. I can jump in the grave and outroar Laertes, but why doesn't somebody put the finger on who is keeping Pound there and why? Who is on the receiving end, for instance, of "A Poet's System of Economics"? Signor Uberti's "fond memories" are fine, but if I had been locked up for— what? ten years?—I believe I might get a little bored with the peace that passeth understanding. I guess I still don't understand what the hell it's all about, tho' one hears various versions . . . .

Read quite evidently does not reciprocate your̄ sentiments: his latest collection of essays has one on "Poetic Diction," which among others contains the following sentence: "It was with the school which Hulme started and Pound established that the revolution begun by W'worth was finally completed." If you ask me that's quite a collocation. First place, I can't see Hulme as having *started anything* established by you. Or really started anything at all. As I see it, he got some interesting ideas from Bergson and wrote about five very trivial setting up exercises later than your rhythm (which owed nothing to theory) had declared itself. As to W'worth, that strikes me as a meaningless way of paying tribute to whatever new freedom it was you found. If I had to say it, I'd put the proposition in some such way as:

France	Chaucer	Cathay	Pound
	England		England

But I don't want to take anything away from Read's obviously sincere admiration for your verse, which I'm sure he understands much better than I do, as well as being in an incommensurably stronger position to PLACE it historically. Frost would describe Hulme to me as though he were a bit of a bully. He (Frost) repeatedly told story of encountering Hulme and being asked, "Why haven't you been around? I've kicked out all those hangerons you met" and how he boasted, "They won't kill me, I'm much too important" before they drafted him and Jerry winged him instanter.

Incidentally, I don't know if you knew Frost after he had become no slouch as a bully himself, thanks to the adulation of thirty years of women's clubs. He was, did I mention, my colleague at Amherst, foul village if there ever was, and I'm afraid never forgave me for clean forgetting a luncheon invitation. I recall how he wd derive what seemed to me an incongruous type of mirth from stories surrounding your kindness in getting his *Boy's Will* published for him. Moral—don't help future idols. That sort of New England finger-on-the-side-of-the-nose—do you suppose it occupied any place in the world for which manners were prescribed by the *Li-Ki*??

Especial thanks for mention of Goullart. My (??) Brunton is Paul and if he was an Egyptologist I am Bishop Sheean. I confessed that as scholar and/or stylist he is a mess. Kingsland could well be Florence Farr's man: certainly sounds like.

Current's strong suit, on a snap judgment, looks like representing decadence and deliquescence as conspiracy. I still think the point about Jews was best made in *Merchant of V*, when Xianity excommunicated bankers as such (right?), so the Jew assumes the role much as that caste (forget the name) was delegated to handle the ordure in India, with psychological consequences to be expected. So they are born with a curse, predictably scramble for grades in my classes, etc., etc. Can't see why one of the greatest living champs for the insulted and injured shd want to make trouble for them. I'd lay odds they'll do more to spring you than the Italians. Just a hunch. I never REALLY was in Europe till last summer when I fell in love with Spain and thought my own land a most unhappy one.

PROSODY. I suppose the *Inferno* does "articulate a total sound," like the *Matthew Passion*; but they both live in the cadences, many of which my late friend Antonio Borgese seemed glad to skip when we read it. No one could ever arrive at ANOTHER wholeness by listening to you, and no one can imitate yours. D.H. Lawrence said, "Scanned verse is dead in 50 years," but I see no signs. Without measure most of us would have to give up, but then perhaps we should.

I have quite adopted the Sandbag nomenclature. Unwilled affec. from

JT

P10 / TLS   **14**

17 June '57

PURRzicely/ Hulme's notes pubd/ 1927 did not have immense
repercussions on people who had not read 'em in the 19 tteeens
etc/ <in 1917> Herbie's racket. didn't he ediTUM ???

I have been fairly meticulous in acknowledging debts / DEEP ones to
       Ford for example/

in Ron Duncan's mag/ believe I did a rectifica "This Hulme business"

       H's REAL value as policeman keeping down fleet st
animalculae too valuable to bury under a phoney legenda.

Frost got a nacherl streak of N. Eng. meanness/
his rural rumpus better than what was in mags (Harry Kemp etc. in 1910)

       WOLLER TOOT.

Believe Chao has no end of degrees / Chink professorships etc. before
commies slaughtered/ etc.

           still keeping quiet cause relatives in reach
of the Rooseveltian Dex White gang in China.

Read, phoney anarchy for parlour use / wont come clean on
historic data, *ergo* dull.

Possum showing signs of life, but dont YET see Nieb/ is spittin on
sacrament, but does ask for context.

           in fact may be chance of revival/
whether he will consent to pubctn/ of *King Bolo*, I dunno.

Is Alan Watts the louse did a bk/ on me or is that some other plural ??

W. Watt, singular, I mean watt in singular, youth of some promise.
<Ciardi precisely as sez J.T.>

Chao/ god damn it ENGLISH METRIC / the crumps at Harvard holding
up my diagrams of the SOUND of the Kung-thology/

more to be learned there than from Arnaut Daniel/ possibly/

anyhow since I did Arnaut none of the bloody scrougers has done **any** WORK

Now the boys in S. Paolo are going on from Mallarmé and Rimb/ on Vowels.

Write N.H. Pearson, 233 H.G.S. Yale Station, N.Haven CONN/ game
       for data re Chao

What is keeping me in here is JEWS/ B.Baruch/ Winchell "E.P. out over
my (i.e. Winchell's) dead body." Javitz Ike's latest confessor and
light/ who

set up howl over Bubblegum award AFTER the kike commies in S.America
    howled/

None but commies had zense to observe that *Cantos* are a POLITICAL implement
like the *Div. Com.*

      (vs. temporal power) or Shx Hizzeries/

Charlie lost his noggin 33 years after Wm. Shx demise.
        <& objection to unlimited monarchy>

and down you relapse into any idea that *Current's* mild restatement
is due to passivity.

Unless you are ready to read some history/ distinct from the brainwash
handed out by the hired beanerOcracies/

                you take it grampaw has been
on this since 1915.

        just like <gen.> del Valle gettin it from <adm.> Beatty:
        war over

yu yanks going home, politicians going Versailles to start next one."

Hell yes, you can talk theology <to E.P.>/ I probably read as much
Migne as you have

cert/ more than they wd/ give you in a protestant theolog/ beanery

let us say Jale puttin out 2 Niebuhrs/ with allergy to exact use of
words.

Yu'l thank me for Goullart when yu git it.

Ambrose on the way. slow post

    Wotchu know re/ Andrew D.White ? of whom I just hear with time lag.

To confute Bob McA/ who said I wrote of a murka that never wuz.

benedictions. White rather clear re/ woptaly pre 1870/

                                              EP

have you ever read any *Talmud?* there are some extracts available
I think Mr. Friedman or some such ebraiologist has printed a few.

data if wanted.

or looked into KAHAL SYSTEM in Hroosia?
remember the *Protocols* were printed in 1919/ famous libel suit reversed
but yu never hear it was REVERSED. C.H.D. remarked: if not the outline
of a conspiracy, must have been writen by someone with gift of prophecy
never claimed fer the prophets of old. all yu got do is
correlate events AFTER 1919.

Main crime/ reading 10 vols Morgenthau *Treasury* Reports sent me

---

Remainder of above letter missing.

15

Dear E.P.   *June 21*

To yrs of 17 June.

"This Hulme Business." I obtained this and was floored by the "two great men" "inspected" there. *Twentieth Century Lit.* will (this month) print my "New Reflections on the *Golden Bowl*," rather a nasty attack on James, I guess. Hudson I ever loved this side idiotry, like he was my father or Rich. Jefferies or Poynings in the Sussex Downs, minus my father's low I.Q., or J's mumbojumbo or the flapdoodle about Sussex. Would rather have known him than any (other) of your generation or his, perhaps. I recall being directed by a hostile cop to Epstein's shrine, scarcely in keeping with Rima.

R. Niebuhr. I first arrived in NYC with the England theolog fellowship before I got out of all that. Niebuhr was on my board of examiners for the S.T.M. (Master of Sacred Theol) conferred reluctantly for profane essay on B.Croce. Niebuhr swung quite an ax with the students qua so-called "social gospel." Hot Bosche preacher in the big time who blushed easy. His calvinistic utterances are, as Byron says, "writ in a manner which is my abhorrence." Did he ever experience deity? Others too are troubled by spiritual cataract but are less noisy. Interesting friendship between Niebuhr and my old classmate Auden!

Who is King Bolo? Do you mean Eliot has its disposal? Many allusions in this letter that get away from me. Have I heard of Javitz? I thought Ike liked clowns like Godfrey and Wilson. I once had an opinionated N.T. prof who could chatter in fluent Hellenic name of Charles Harold Dodd, otherwise wdnt know "C.H.D." What is WOLLER TOOT? (Humorless me here, I doubt not) Is Kahal a talmudic apochypha? Andrew White also ignotum. Bob McA—MacArthur? Temper the wind, dear correspondent.

Alan Watts might conceivably have his lousy phase at that, but I'm rather confident he has written only on Zen & such. I see he just resigned from the Amer. Inst. of Asiatic Studies in San Francisco; I wondered if because Ernest Wood, Vedantist, saw past him. wot other watt assailed pound? Best book I know on Zen is an odd sort of anthology called *Zen in English Literature* and Oriental Classics by R.H. Blyth, obscure prof at Tokyo (Hokuseido Press '48). A. Huxley only one I know who knows this, puts it where I do.

Anything available on ENGLISH METRIC that you had anything to do with is for me. Do you mean Harvard is holding it up? Again you got me . . . . All right, so "Herbie" is dull. He seems to understand Klee, that sort of thing, has read more than the rest. I assure you I am not accustomed to addressing myself uninvited to my ex-countrymen knighted for letters, but I was once moved to ask Read to state the difference between Whitman and . . . I forget what highly wrought prose. He answered by return: " . . . a quantum leap." I thought that was pretty bright. I guess it arose from something in his book on style. And I always thought his *In Defence of Shelley* contra Eliot's—(*illegible word*) was, if pedestrian, valid as well as valorous for anyone to stick his neck out for Percy . . . .

Small point: whether you wd say my impression of Stein was correct, since she was perhaps too clever for me at Amherst (Goddamst) that time. She had a deaf act, kept saying "what" in a queer faint voice. Her favorite word was "dead." "Proust?" "Dead." "Joyce?" "Dead." "Pound?" "Dead." So then I said, "Miss Stein, is there anybody now writing who is alive?" — "What?" This question I then repeated real loud and she said (her words): "There is Stein." It seemed to me then (1936) and still that she wrote herself out with the partly functional *Making of Americans*, thereafter jumped on her own bandwaggon. No? (Why bring it up when I don't give a damn?)

I will write Pearson merely because you say so, but repeat: a) my influence outside my own dept is zero; b) all appointments are made for academic year 1957-8 at SDSC, as at Penn, Hamilton and the rest of our venerable "beaneries" (Love that). I trust now you will tip me off re any action committee to establish that if Pound is nuts I am Bishop Sheen. Do you have any fun in the "bgzz"? Music? Friends? Need anything procurable? . . . Just prying from pathos.

Yrs.,

J.T.

P11 / TLS

16

J.T.

25 Giugno '57

herewith coHerent statement re/ Chao
on seParate sheet.

Notes and glossary/ in reply J.T.'s of 21st inst.

Yes, *Evviva* Hudson / saw him but once/ elicited one. possibly 2 letters
You are dead right re/ value.

amicitia/ Niebuhr-Auden arouses no incredulity on part of yr/ present
correspondent.

MS/ of Bolo entrusted to me by its author years ago. a fictitious
african monarch with *Anschauung* as might then have been
evolved neath the Harvard elms, if that's where the elms
are.

Cant remember prenom of the Watts who did a lousy book on yr/ present
correspondent / I spose it is listed somewhere.

voilà tout (purrnounced with a *w* (non teutonic) and the final *t*)
as champZ elíZAH

or "Wagner"? Oh you mean "the sleepink-car man."

re/ possession a *palazzo* in Venice. I dare say
I was indicating the wrong palace. and not sure if IS the Vendramin

My impression of Gertie (and of Amy) one globular in form, the other
pyramidal in construction.

neither necessary to the evolution
of the city of Dioce, or the new PAIdeuma.

"et th pvice I paidt for 'em I ken afford tuh keep 'um"

(re/ the Picassos and the Cézanne).

hysterical appeal to deliver a y.m. who has been rushed to N.York
by a hysterical chew and his starving ma / now (the y.m.
presumably aryan) in danger (as d.g.'s correspondent seems to think) of
lobotomy)

If either d.g. or HIS hysterical correspondent had made
clearer exposition of the facts, I might refer them to J.T. but would
not.

One congressman seems to be getting relative items into the
"extension" of the Congressional record / which publication is NOT

on sale at the Capital news stands / but in small pp/ several pages
from the end (of the daily issue, or <of> some daily issues)
   does reveal HOW and where in the Keppertl a persistent enquirer
      COULD get a copy.

/ if this parenthesis seem to have been ABruptly introduced, it is
to save circumlocution. *i.e.* NOT a question of whether you are
Bishop Sheen

          BUT of whether any coherent adults in the wreckage of
our republic

          can sufficiently cohere to agree on some clauses of the
constitution/

notably one re/ hab/ corpus/ being suspended only in case of invasion
or rebellion when pubk/ safety demands it.

Do you recall any INVasion of the U.S. eleven or 12 years ago / ??

I mean to say: what is the use discussing subjective confusions
of individuals

          UNLEss at least a working minority of our concitoyens
starts taking an interest in government, legal and constitutional.

a Roman correspondent writes: *dallo scontro dogmatico, siamo già alla
crisi pragmatista.*

but my beloved daughter finds that he tends to git distracted
from issues of *consiglio communale* by her *treccie bionde.*

In other words *if* sob stuff re/ ME can lead to any clarity
    in civic thought,

              go on and SOB

But didn't you while in theology hear about Paul (they got the habit of
altering names, Paul *né* [or intermediately] Saul) was litigious.

   Mr Joyce used to sing *"dey got dat toilet*
               frum Pontius Poilate."

(earlier lines of the strophe)
              "That judges on the bench are foRRced to wear
        A nightgown and a bob-wig made
             of someone else's hair."

          pardon laconism, I meant merely to
forward the Chao information.

                       yrs *EP*

17

June 29, 1957

Twelth epistle of EP to hand ("*25 Giugno*"). Earlier ones are a mistake to
refer back to, their extreme compression insuring too many unanswered
suggestions, not therefore ignored. Thus, "May 16" letter contained a
short list of those who had "put it in the right place": 8 names, only 5 of
which clicked since I missed on Erigena, R. St. Victor, & Rémusat.
Nothing the matter with batting better than 600 on a Pound reading
list . . . . Hope you didn't think silence re your mention of Wyndham
Lewis, for example, put me among those ignorant of the role AND thing-
in-itself of *Tarr*, not to speak of *Time & Western Man*. I teach Contemp.
Lit. as being almost entirely (often boringly) obsessive with the Time
rumpus—more recently hipped on Space. I have often wondered how
Lewis escaped being tarred himself with the subtler infections of the
British thing. I'd better not talk, since Limeyism in disguise is too like the
other odors our best friends won't tell us about, tho' one is wont to assume
a lucky unction from divine birthplace.

Your current missive is less cryptic for me than the last. I don't remember
and can't find any overt ref to Venice, unless Wagner had a summer beach
cabin there or something. And is "d. g." one of EP's noms?? It looks here as
tho' said d. g. was on the receiving end of an appeal he toyed with ringing
me in on to rescue an imminent victim (fellow patient?) from surgical
mayhem, or is this all wet? I appear to have less trouble with
abbreviations and impounded spellings (found myself wondering how
much of this Joyce caught from you) than with the initials jag. You still
haven't elucidated H.C.D. As you were: C.H.D.?? (Possibly unimportant).

Returning to the one before the last. There is some evidence for the
assumption that Lit has lost some of the interest you have felt forced to
bestow on politics, and I try to make allowance for the extreme
unlikelihood that literary concerns that burned for you half a century ago
are going to light up for you all over again because some goddamned
college professor who tinkers (however seriously) with the craft sounds
you out on this and that with a Boswellian (?) light in his eye. Well, it shd
go without saying that "Forget it" is a standing order, and you don't even
have to read what follows, let alone comment: It is that I am still trying to
digest the POLITICAL threat of Dante, Sh'sp, & Pound. I believe I'd rather
avoid the bait on the bard, if only because I can't help doubting that his
impact was felt in 33 years, least of all by the bloody congregationalists

who had Chuck's "noggin." With Dante, let's say it was as you say, or I would'nt know if not. Pound. Isn't it entirely too early?

At present the *Cantos* seem to be setting up almost as many different interpretations as readers, as witnessed by that compendium on you—forget what it was called. My own reading of the *Cantos*, for instance, might turn out to resemble yours about as closely as B. Jonson reading J'son would resemble that dramatist being read by — ? — some neophyte of his period (afraid I don't have Yeats' trick of picking the right previous "body of fate" or whatever for myself!). When I personally EMBARK (perfect word for it) on the first *Cantos,* the chief symptom of the experience is the constant effulgence of the naked Adriatic and Aegean sun. Until your foot begins to weigh down on the pedal entry and then, tho' I can see considerable hell let loose and history is all *there,* and no commie, of course, can afford to enjoy any version of history distinct from his own grubby little version of it, still I just don't believe they would know what it was hit them, not the commies I have known . . . .

St. Ambrose arrived from the Digger. Thanks a million. I wonder how the hell the good father knew all about that. If my Latin was less rusty, I'd probably know already, but I will, I will. Digging is just a GREAT deal more funereal a process for this one.

J.T.

18

Swb/ 1Lug/Andrew D. White, Autobiography (Century Co, N.Y.
N.Y, 1905/ very instructive.
ever hear of bk/ "Progress of Morals" by Fowler of Corpus Christi
who deplored Hegel/ sometime pre 1885.

White met Mommsen, otherwise keen of history as writ/ by them
that hadn't dug below the surface, Tho he (A.D.W.) did dig into
some abuses of paper money. Interesting ? that he adored Grotius
/ whom I spose I shall have to look at, if you don't.
ties in with addenda Mensdorf added to my notes on real causes
of war / sent to Nic Smeary Butter (Carnegie Hoaxtitoot) in 1927
in endeavor to stir that otiose body and bastard. Mary
hunting for copy, success not reported. NO contacts YET
with any History Depts/ in u.s. beaneries / Lit. Profs. unlikely
to be able to git stews/ to pry into archives of the Floundation.
/ of course nowt there to indicate the collaboration on part of <y.v.t.>
. . . Mensdorf, as loyal to Habsburg's omitted ref/ to
dynastic introgues/ BUT he was right as they were then obsolete /
the Fatty Can wangles not falling exactly into that cat/g/
tho I suppose the Bankhaus Pacelli and similar *cloacae* still
tangle.

AT any rat Groot appears to have opposed Calvin. White thinks him
root of Hague tribunal, and that he (White) helped Bülow to get it
started.

Converge/ or vtx, last week.
Agresti/ rehabilitating Augustine/ with qt. re Memory
RR. Frank Lloyd Wright, <Lao Tze> on architecture, not the walls
        but the living space.
Stock/ Albertus de la Magna/ pre Agassiz.
kid named Chas. Martell going to bat for E.P.
H. Comfort (latin, Haverford) who remembers old White sez: one of
few books that ought to be longer not shorter.
Light on Tolstoi's muddle. old believers (russia) naturally
disgusted when iggnorant apes wanted cross (sign of) made with
three fingers (two for dual nature Xt) also the IMBecility
of *filioque*. (Anselm having noted a sane trinity).
White sane on liquor control among 50 other items.
ALL religious fuss probably due to sheer ignorance plus profit
motive / STEWpidity of some ½ educated buggar mucking with

some simple and obvious bit of KOINE ENNOIA/
Anselm, Rémusat (Chas.) philos of common sense, Herb.
of Cherbury.

present jew filth in —space travel, geophys/ year/
worse than C.H.D.'s quote "eyes in ends of the earth."
          with fake yeast, fake wheat etc. *hic est*
medium mundi.
White's vol/ on War <*of*> science <*vs Theology*>/ evidently
some opposition: rise of man, fall of man.
Orig. sin. another ignorance/ perverted from gk/ idea
of PARTIC. crime having consequence. Atreides, etc.
Boris sound: left universal of all man, for tribal gawd
<*or*> punk of the hebes. Sd/ it re/ Milton in Spurt of Romance
in 1910 as from earlier perception.

P13 / TLS

19

J. Theob: 2 *Lug*/ the foregoing to participate
you into corresp/ with the Rev. H. Swabey
Rathby Rectory, Louth, Lincs. England
Hem/ and MacLeish been on firing line, timing their releases
and Hem at least running ahead of what wd/ pass copy desks.

/ Possum has been solicitous/ very at first, and has signed recent
evangelical to the punks/ etc. I dont think he TRIES to keep his
mind closed, I think it just nacherly IS that way. Swallows ANY
filth any damn official tells him. Conscience re/ betrayal of Mihaelovitch
but OBTUSE (*vide his scripta*) re moral turpitude and growth of same.
Failed to understand my picture of mind of england, as in *Cantos*
XIV/XV. nacherly names not included, BUT several identifiable/
and having told Polish damblastador in '39: "God help you if you
trust England." Might now note that I did not wait to note a few
defects even in 1919. Some of the viler <*damn'd*> weren't then in
public light.
Now dealing in DEETail with J.T.'s of 29 ult. C.H.D(ouglas) father of
Social Credit/ dambrits pretended it warnt there/ Gugg "Gregory" of
London SPEWL of Econ/ falsified C.H.D.'s statement, Bible Bill
in Alberta mixed with a perversion or horrible exaggeration of Gesell,
which Bankhead swallowed/
BUT Alberta being under central Canadian
usurers NEVER had free hand to practice . . . but DID force mention of
idea, and do some good.
Did yu see the horrible kike <on TV> out for space travel?
satellites/ etc. to keep mind off rotten bread and frog bakers bypassing
yeast?
d.g. Gordon. *vid. Ac. Bul.* NO JT not expected to get into
THAT tangle <*P.S. This a.m. another rotted family wanting to put kid in jew
asylum to kikitize.*>. merely list of morning distractions. Dant vs/ Temporal
Power (ref also AD White). FACT is Chas/ lost his diseased head
33 years post Shx. AND Homer, Dant, Shx were CONCERNED with economics.
Homer pre-monetary, but . . .
am merely fighting the bunshoppe and artyshoppe
boys/ re/ RIGHT of bard to mention serious subjects. WHether he can
ketch the konscience of the kink or merely poke Polonius in the jibblets.

as to interpreters/ last was in Krautland/
"leave the Duke go for Gold"

the enemy; telling 'em Duke is a cigarette. Eva NOT having
connected with Wilkes re/ Wellington.
            let us return to kummrad kumminkz': sadist! you try to
make people think.
            A mewzicial <bloke> noted something between earlier parts
            and Pisans/
Rapallo music laboratory, and dechifrage of 20 Vivaldi concerti, reducing
to make possible performance for fiddle and piyanny
NO memory for music/ have some sense of quality. No use ref/ to
particular bits/ Rossini trained by copying *Haydn* parts.
                        enc. noozitem from woptaly.
Some wops read greek in Ambrose time/ Forget if Ammianus or where
there is ref/ to Alex and brahmin/ wot about Apollonius Tyana,
something there also. sombud wrut his *vita*.

                                    yrz
Apochryph, I shd/ say as Amb/ sounds more as if he had Roman arena
in mind, than Macedon . . .

    / point of which interpolation IS that I dont feel any PERSONAL
need of any more metaphysics, or anybody elses metaphysics BUT
do feel my job is to keep a few peoples attention directed toward
IMMEDIATE needs/
            vs/ atom bomb/ space manias/ Xtn (giudeo Xtn
—perceived at 16) MANIA/ the one command of these DAMNED *Anschauungs*:
            Thou shalt attend to thy neighbors business before
thou attendest to thine own.
Crushing of ALL local civilizations in favour of uniformity and
central tyranny.
Alzo, attempt to stop ALL study of nature <*veget & animal*>/ which is study
of
VARIETY
            Yeats had a few decent ideas / one of 'em: the new sacred book of
the arts.
AND text books could be aimed thatta way.

Flaubert's *sottisier* was useful. My "studies in contemporary mentality"
has never got reprinted, though MacLuhan tried to continue the fight.
this is the negative or destructive part of the shindy.

But the problem of timing, of what shall be told the pupil first
            is of INTEREST.

When they stopped SHOWING the best, and perverted composition
into what they call "creative writing"
                        there was a slump/
progressive decay.

                as parallel from Condé Nast, hunting for contents
to catch ads.

Ever see "A Daughter of Confucius"

                        by Su-Ling Wong

worth the price, cause she notes SHE was started on
        "The nature of man is good"

English primer gave kids: The cat saw the rat.

                                ad interim.

                                                        EP

Having now FOUND yr/ epistle/ I will read the KrishnaM if I ever
get hold of it (or read at it).

    And if yu knew all about Vincent did you THEN consider he cd/
learn anything he didn't already want to know? If it is THAT Vincent.
of Chicago.

T7
20

To EP of 7/2   Jy 6, '57

Hard for me to pick up what you and Swabey were settling, esp. what had
weight re 3 fingers versus 2. I shd think Jesus cd make do with 2. As I had
it figured the most persistent and least resistant-to-intelligence of the
Xian notions came thro' the Vedic Indians from the Iranian Mitra, Varuna
& Agni, the 3 eyes of the Illuminator. Varuna=G the Father, Creator,
putting on sky substantial, etc.// (Mazda) Agni mediator between men and
gods, hymns call "friend", bringing gods down to sacrifice, etc.=J.C.,
unless the Galilean (as I happen to prefer) was another avatar like
Krishna, Confucius and quite a few more scattered about.// Mitra="Holy
G"?? defender of truth, also mediator between Mazda and man, giving of
course name to religion fr which Xters took Eucharist, etc. etc. . . . . Your
translations in the Square $ Series are doing more for me than anything I
have run across in a long time. . Needless to say, when I speak of
"esotericism" I don't have in mind anything covered by the magnificent
crack on p. 9 about "poking into magic." How do you bring Kung's vision
of CHARACTER home to a senator? If you can't who can, and they have you
locked up, in more senses than one. Hearing about these people making
motions (H'way, MacLeish, Martell) will make me lonesome till they
circularize.

Further refs to "Possum" serve as come-on, which despite "declassifi-
cation" by EP, I shd probably be smart to passup. Here I *could* have a
warp, since when I first started to practise aestheticism (Oxf), his was the
only voice (none of us knowing then that he got it from you). Myself, to
my then disadvantage no doubt, pinned the flag to a belligerent
incantatory (neo Kelleyandsheets) mast and was in a minority of one, the
only one with that smell that they even bothered to be rude to. Well, all
that passed off, including recriminations. But when you use the word
"swallow" of him, you start something. I'm not talking about presence or
absence of hygienic qualities in what goes down; it's the swallowing
itself, the jumping on the sturdiest bandwagon in sight, or 's how it looks.
That evening in N'hampton, Mass., he sat on a couch with a priest,
resembling a public *in flagrante delicto*, except the nooky was sins being
confessed, looked like. (I was just curious enough to sneak up on them. It
wasn't sins exactly. They were giving a solemn rundown on the local
shrines, this being Sat night, to find which one was temperamentally
compatible for the morrow morn, just spiky enough but not too much.) So

there it is. There are the 4 *Quartets*. No vision. All belief and pitch tuned to go with, or rather that's the way I feel about it. This was of no use to my generation, less still to the one coming up. Can't understand it. He cd have got there with about two "heaves," as you make Kung say, where we'll have to take a thousand. As I have observed the symptoms in people I have known well, it results from an inability, as Americans say, to "take it." The horror of having to think it through is too much. End of again having talked out of turn . . .

. . . These periodic lobotomies, "kikitrizations," etc. sound ghoulish enough, what goes? And yes we have TV finally. Kids. No way not, except banish them. Don't recall any connection here with space travel and your pals, tho' speaking of generations I'm a child of mine with any old corn about green queens on Venus and come for more, provided it isn't slanted like the thinly disguised tractates of C.S. Lewis, who pinch-hit for my tutor A.J. Carlyle (Econ. of the Middle Ages), already then (*i.e.*, Lewis) showing first sinister spasms of fideism.

Yrs. J.T.

P14 / TL
21

J.T.   10 Lug/

Interruption of correspondence / G.I. Jim Stevens,
. . . poEM on elefant good enuf
for Stock to print, *Edge* 5, I think, anyhow *Edge*/
just been in, out of hours, distressed that his life has been SAVED
by refusal of Harvard to have him.

I have suggested San Diego State/
I dunno that yu wil thank me/ you cd/ at least indicate which courses
least deleterious/

//

Kuan Tzu/ ever heard of Lewis Maverick, S.Illinois Univ. evidently
enough funds to print well.

looks to me most useful contrib/ to life of mind in
occident since Frobenius.

Worth perusal in last decade. De Angulo, "Indians in Overalls."
Waddell/Rock/Goullart "Forgotten Kingdoms."

now the Kuan (Chung) Tzu

(seven bucks). Different level of mind, and educ/ as cf/
the bible thumpers/

anyhow, I don't delay the glad tidings. EU-which what.
Gruesen, who bust

the incommunicado @ Pisa with a message from
Santayana (*i.e.* Col. in charge a minor haavud prof/ cdn't resist G.S.)
sd/ Greusen in yester/ thesis on Jung and Schopenhauer which he thinks
FINISHES off Jung/

leZOPE . . .

Father D'Arcy sd/ to have purrsuaded N. Car. to be about to print it.
appear that "The Point" is run by Feeny ex-Soc.J.

but does quote Ambrose.

reckon yr/ Trinity is what old Pisani ("archivesc/ attached to Vat/ Soil")
tried to sell me/

he had been apostolic delegate to India.
also prof. of Econ/ before that.

idea in XIV/XV Canters was that much of the identity had eroded/

non raggiamo di lor / BUT at least one of 'em has since seemed to fill specific-
ations
  others who deserve that ambience hadn't been heerd tell on
in 1919.
Satisfaction of having told Patocki in '39, it was unwise to trust
  a certain power.

P15 / TLS   **22**

22/ July/ foregoing evidently lost in excitement re/ the KUAN-TZU
seems Lewis Maverick is on sick leave in Calif/ hope they haven't
pizon'ed him for revelation of crapularity of all history as taught
in occidental , Vaticand or otherwise brainwashed beaneries for past
300 years/
How far are you from Los Angeles? his address
            2027 Bentley Av. Los Ang. 25.

     Difference in state of mind of man brought up on Kuan and the
Four Books, and the lousiness of mentality
            reared on irresponsible civic
anarchy /
       wot yu call Xters /
Whether the fugg at Yale know they are acting as agent for
     what Maverick managed to print in Illinois, gornoze.
I enclose N.H.P.'s comment/
anyhow, the *Kuan Tzu* is worth $7/. Far Eastern Publications
            26 H.G.S. Yale.
sorry to have lost thread of exchange in excitement re/ horse sense
300 b.C.

                       ever yrs
                       E. P.

T8   **23**

Dear E.P.

Sorry, sickness here — the little tike with a big germ, which inevitably he
gave to his da and it took my quack to pull me out. I call him a quack
because he stands outside the approved pale, but in consideration of how
very few orthodox MD's are on the level I use the term strictly as an
honorable distinction.

Yes I heard from "James Stephens" (my first thought being, "Thought that
little leprechaun was caput"). His letter was a riot. I tried to get the point
over that I own the distinction of being one of the very few in history who
have for a short while succeeded in bamboozling EP. Since then I haven't
heard from him. Is he married? solvent? Our only extra bed is shortly
to be taken by a Hungarian student (also hungry) but we have various
camping facilities. Must say I have had the best luck with musicians and
even near musicians — for reasons not surprising. Hope the enclosed
from MacLeish will not prove more disconcerting than nothing at
all . . . . Good for Frost to get off his but(t).

Shall certainly have the college libr go after Maverick's KUAN TZU, which
sounds like one good deed in a naughty world.

And who is NHP? — aside from being a reader of *Poetry*, Chic, which
latterly, as I believe I said , leaves me out. Ralph J'son sent them a
demolishing broadside on Kenner which they didn't print, so there must
be a tie-up of some sort.

I wd want to see what Greusen has on Jung. From my standpoint, merely
to have cut Freud down to size is something. And the "racial unconcious"
when taken out of its *deutsch* jargon and relieved of its inaccuracies of
thought strikes me as a necessary lead. As for Schop., what other
metaphysical aesthetic is there that isn't too boring to read (I once had to
read them all in the line of business)? I am allowed to guess that Greusen
will live solely for the Pisan gesture.

O yes. Do you ever see our so conscious (?) comic sheet, *New Yorker*?
Their June 22 number has a long thing by Anthony West (natural son of
H.G. and Rebecca, I guess) on Japan which I think might interest you.
Did I mention my Japanese friend, the poet Ichiro Kono. He and I together
have been working on a collection of modern Japanese poets (Englishing
them). Aside from the fact that their poets seem to have an unusually high
incidence of insanity (I mean reflected in the poetry), they repay a second

look, and some of them even in English make our current crop look moribund. I note that Kono treats my Zen leanings with a sort of affectionate disdain. His loss.

Pisani? What kind of archivist is that? If I told you who seems to me to know most about trinities you wd laugh and laugh. Some people, some authors and such, just get LEFT — how long for, I wonder? They say, *Magna est veritas*, etc. but it is my observation that the truth shows little interest in being known but just narcissistic-like in itself.

Most of the things I was going to mention have slipped away . . . . We are going to camp for a while, if we can all get over this bug.

Tout à vous,
John T

P16 / TL

24

J.T.

Ag/ 3

Had not remotest intention of thrusting the flustered Stephens

onto you as house guest / Yes. he has nuptuated, apparently without
calamity/ in fact an improve/ possible couples being so DAMN much
rarer than admissible singles.

N.H.P. *vide* Sq $/ advisory / Pearson of Yale, *vid* intelligent note on
Agassiz somewhere in front or bk matter of one Sq/

Maverick just as good as his book/ even apparently willing to enter
into conversation with other denizens.

I can lend yu copy of Grueson/ but doubt if it is necessary reading
matter/ so damn much else that ALL of us need to know *more/*

Merely saw that West had done a Rebecca / but not DEEvoted to
either of 'em/ tho R/ had her points / and H.G. was amusing the
few times I met him.

Vid/ quote re/ bitch on monument at beginning of
some canto or other/

believe concordance promised/ until which
must leave ubicities to Kenner/

passionate struggle of K–pupil, deepchested of
fatherland/ with Eva/

misprint. it shd/ read "bag of Duke's."
both schools of interpretation wrong, but Ken/ philologically the
more so.

Rotocalcos mostly reach bughouse in time, donated with kindly
intentions.

I used not to get Yeats' disgust with ALL weekly and
monthly publications/

alzo *Harpers* in 1878 or '9/ obit of Agassiz, level of decency
of that era

inducing to decay post Condé Nast/ nation hooked to
habit of NOT reading books FIRST.

Edg/ to print list of reading matter obtainable in paper backs/
if yu come on anything good, yu might mention in letters / NOT
suggesting you look for it/ merely if it turns up.

Woodward's General Grant / is in Premier.
Brooks Adams 1.25 somewhere. making supplementary list
collateral, not necessarily curricular, reading.

main system is that of vile Reese/ continental post Tauchnitz. Nos. 1-2
Ulysses / did NOT want anything else grade A.
"Germans like to THINK they are cultured, if they see *Ulys*/ at start,
will THINK the other items on list are literature."
                    O *talmud* where ends thy filthery.

2/various reaches to ruin *Traxiniai* in purrformance/ You might
tell Ichiro the one thing I most want to go INTO jap/ is *Trax*/

Only Minoru or the other Noh co/ are fit to do it.

A miss Lust eggzited at Ron Duncan's BRIGHT idea of Cocteau decor/
(which wd/ be desirable detail), but M. Jean has his own eggs to hatch.

Pisani, *arcivescovo* addicted to Vatican Soil.

Got from Anselm a perfectly SANE trinity / *vid* Sq $/ or *koine ennoia*/

INTELLIGENCE, some goes into animal, veg/ min, some dont/

ergo the *filioque* is plain damned idiotic, and only useful when
trying to grab temple lands on eggskeqsz of heresy of possessors.

    Just like "free AND equal" (meant no special privilege IN law court
for nob. or clerg.)

               and term perverted. into antibiologic hogwash
and arsenic.

I didn't know Goullart HAD a yank pubr/

The key word of corruption is: "Nweeee nwant." U.S. Consulate
Paris 1920.

            ngwee nwant 'em awl teh gao bakk.

hope you will git within conversin range some day. Need of reissue of
"il Problema delle Tasse" in wop or yank, greater than -*ianiania*
in retrospect. However that phrase's started 37 years' pilgrimage or *perip-
lum.*

"Seay jeng feller, daon/t yew kno there aint nobody in this
kentry has gaot enny gawDDam rights whatsoever?!"
            Chicago tribunal to Van Dyne, during
Wilsonian era. (not the W.H. Wright pseudonym, a long ex-hollander)

git rid of yr/ bugfections and nJoye the open air of the Sequoias

Theobald being a teacher at a California State College, it was natural that education should be a frequent topic in the correspondence. For Pound of the early years, the value of education had lain in making one "a more complete . . . fuller, more able, more interesting companion" ("Provincialism the Enemy."). Though he never exactly disavowed this view, over the years, as he grew increasingly Confucian, education came to mean something more stripped down and practical—"a preparation for contemporary life," awareness of "immediate needs" and issues (seen, always, by the light of the "classics"), acquisition of knowledge that would translate into action, as opposed to reflection and mere "speculation about." Thus, on August 13, 1957, we find him writing to Theobald:

> no satisfaction till I got to Kung
>   what you DO about it   whicheversodam
> answer you get to the 7 and 77 jabs at unscrewing the inscrutable

And a week or so later

> am not damning all metaphysical speculation/
> St. Bernard/ considerare, investigate/
>   however con-sidera
>   does it fit stars

i.e. of what use is it? Does it help you to sail? Does it advance the agenda?

This was the angle, utilitarian, pragmatic, from which in his middle years he viewed public education in America. He found it for the most part a sham and a disgrace, little more than a mode of national brainwash. The Russians had their Beria program; we had public instruction in irrelevance and triviality, characterized by indifference to history, the classics, and "ALL study of nature, vegetable and animal, which is the study of VARIETY." The block caps here have a more than orthographic interest. What Pound is stressing is discrimination of differences as basic principle not merely of education but of every kind of human activity and association, artistic, scientific, civic, ethnic: "good that hindoos be MORE hindoo," he writes Theobald, "that chinks be MORE chink."

Applied to education this meant not stuffing students with general ideas but teaching them to know particulars, to distinguish creature from creature, idea from idea, word from word. Discrimination, exact terminology ("Ching Ming"), is in fact for Pound, as for Kung, the real and true basis of the State: "if the terminology be not exact, if it fit not the thing" (Kulcher, 16-17) "you cannot conduct business properly . . .," and when people cease to care about such distinctions they are on the way to tyranny, everyone "melted into one stinking pattern." These are matters of primary educational concern for Pound. Hence his stress on turning students' attention outward onto contemporary process and keeping it there, rather than inward upon subjective worlds of the self. Hence, too, his lifelong antipathy to Freudianism and psychiatry: they turn one's attention inward, away from the events of the res publica, and permit public abuses to go unnoticed and unchallenged: "Connect all psychiatry with Beria program" (to Theobald, 8 Sept. '57).

Objectivity vs inwardness (indefiniteness) is everywhere present in Pound, from the early poetic of "hard squares" (Vorticism) vs one of mystery (Symbolism), to his predilection for stampscrip vs the allurements of debt and credit.

Pound was never a sympathetic reader of academic journals, where generalization and abstraction tend normally to abound. When Theobald sends him a copy of Twentieth Century Literature: A Scholarly and Critical Journal (ed. Alan Swallow, Denver, Colorado), containing an article by the sender (on The Golden Bowl), Pound joshingly alludes in his next to "the gulph between J T epistolary, and J T taykin' s pen in 'and." As for the magazine itself (whose lead article had begun, "James Joyce's short story, 'The Dead,' is a morality play in the form of an Aristotelian tragedy" [p. 31]), his comment, if a bit wry, is characteristically candid:

> Swallows cert/ NOT intending to make
> a summer in coloRAdo

But Pound's eye had really been on something bigger, of which the journal in question was only a symptom: "Is there ANY communication," he fires back at Theobald, "between the alarm of E D at what is being swallowed, and the Swallows." True, the alarm of E D (Elizabeth Dilling), sounded in several inflammatory volumes, had been over alleged Jewish infiltration of American financial, political, and educational institutions; yet in spite of that, Pound's chief complaint remains valid—the absence of significant contact, let alone interaction, between thought and government in contemporary America.

He turns next to what he considers a still worse condition, the inferior quality of text books in use in American schools. To open one of them, he writes shudderingly, on August 23, is to "dive into an aquarium . . . full of contagions." This was hardly a momentary fit of exasperation on Pound's part. He had always battled on behalf of sane curricula, elimination of historic "blackout" and "brainwash," study of foreign cultures in, as far as possible, the language of those cultures—all of them central themes, not just of his polemical writings, but of The Cantos (that pedagogical epic, when all is said, on what to read and study), the translations from Chinese and other foreign languages, and many of the literary essays as well. For in spite of his bohemian persona and belligerent attitudes, Pound was a radical classicist who championed a rational and aristocratic conception of art and life, and his rage was almost always over the degradation of values he considered essential to civilization in our time. It was never the merely contemptuous rage of, for instance, his friend Wyndham Lewis, for whom the current state of Western civilization was "a moronic inferno of insipidity and decay," but prophetic rage, full of rectification and construction: "Do this," "Read that," "Look there," "Consider the aim," etc. So it is not very surprising to find him, on Sept. 3, thinking in terms of diving into the "Aquarium" after all, "contagions" or no. Once the plunge was taken, it was only a matter of a few weeks before he and M S (Marcella Spann, a young teacher of English at a Washington Junior College and frequent visitor to St. Elizabeths in those years) had determined the contents of Confucius to Cummings (Pound also sought advice from other readers) and had done most of the notes and miscellanea. For a charming account of the progress of the "Spann-thology," see Marcella (Spann) Booth, "Through the Smoke Hole," Paideuma (Winter, 1974).

25

Aug. 7, '57
(to EP of Aug 3)

I thought I said I told my ex-countrymen to keep the change. No, as far as I know Murray is the only house to date with the moxy to print the forgotten book, and they did come across (don't mind me: there's something in "Ow those cawkney Woyces" (as you put it in yours to Jas Laughlin, Rapallo (?5) January) apropos of *Murd. in Cath:* My Krissz, them cawkney woices) that repels more as I draw further from earshot; and when they use it in a letter, when all I wanted was their book . . . . It's of no consequence. I have it and read it, more than once, and instructed them (enclosing another 3 bucks) to mail another copy to my dear brother in Khartoum, who won't see the resemblance to *The Tempest*, or even perhaps to FAR AWAY AND LONG AGO; nevertheless it will be his meat too. In fact, it looks as tho' he will be separated from his chosen *penates* in the Sudan, much as Goullart. Incidentally, you foxed me, since I said, if I recall, that I was looking for a really satisfactory book on India, and . . . well, it's true, tho' I don't know how you knew it, that while Likiang isn't the political land of my birth, it does SMELL of my Amora memory shocks, again and again, the damndest feeling. Unless one comes across a book like that, and who could expect it, I am reduced to certain dreams — unless I pray Fullbright for a fellowship and make pilgrimage. Well, you know how much I owe. One does not indulge the neural itch of lit. crit. on such a MAN, transport, grief. I shall probably come back to it.

I met H.G. Wells about a year before his death. He insisted on calling me "Tibbald," as tho' I rhymed with ribald, like Pope's victim. I was determined to find out how the hell he had managed to write so much — quantitatively. So I asked him, and he said, "Mr. Tibbald, do you go to the bathroom every day?" I allowed that nature had been kind to me in this respect. "And I," says he, "have to write a little something every day, FOR THE GOOD OF MY HEALTH." I thought Rebecca was quite a gal until I took a dislike to her particular kind of hot breath. One can fancy the presence of the strain in the natural son; but I think he has something a little better.

Traxiniai?? Impart and I'll tip off Kono.

Reese???

K-pupil; Eva; "bag of Duke's": also got away, so I didn't do so well this time.

Back to first things. WHERE IS GOULLART? Holing out in Singapur? He not only bore a charmed life those 9 years but must do so still, or the commies wd have got him for that book. They can't let that sort of disdain stay loose in the world.

J.T.

P17/TLS   **26**

13 Ag/57 J.T.

Rock answers, knows more Na Khi than Goullart but hasn't packaged it
so conveniently/
                    bilingial edtns/ of the very fine poetry of Na Khi etc.
Without *Muan pbo.* (sacrifice to heaven) no reality.
        Goullart don't answer, or hasn't to date/ no address save care his
pubrs/
Naturally fed UP with all Yeats, Blavat, etc. not impressed with Coomara
swami in person.
               any more than I was by T.H. Lawrence
               neither seeming to get the
grip on specific specimens of ART.
no satisfaction till I got to Kung/
             what you DO about it   whicheversodam
answer you get to the 7 and 77 jabs at unscrewing the inscrutable.
Believe I HAVE covered most points raised in yrs/ to "Dear Mark"
somewhere or other in my published conglomerates.
Yes, that was about Wells' level. Only had one long talk with him
apart a FEW meetings at tay pawtiez
I was trying to scrouge some currency for Joyce / later a few
frivolous letters from the riviera / I fergit about what.
I was probably trying to get him to come clean on some econ/ item.
Anyhow too many real writers that I WANT to read, tho I hate
reading as a process/
             only do it to putt a dent in my iggurunce.
Was it you or the admirable Maverick who said he would actually
MEET and converse with other fauna now parked in Calif??
Carsun Chang's book on neO-kung due, I think Chao said, in Oct.
effect of bhud infiltration, leading to Zen.
Reese, the s.o.b. that started the post-Tauchnitz continental edn/
paper backs (?penguin or zummat)
Eva/ my german traductrix/ refs to my own output, sometimes
comprehensible to correspondents, but not REQUIRED as part
of correspondent's *paideuma.*

She has done a nobl/ introd to *ABC des Lesens,* quoting Dag H/
etc.

the aim being to spring grampaw someday, when the
level of WHite House kulch proceeds, as from Mickey Rooney under
OOOzenstein the damned to Irv. Berlin under the kewpie doll.

Junzaburo is in *Edge* No 5 (or zummat) all vivid japs and
traductions of, shd. go to Melbourne.

Heaven knows what Stock will find for future issues. Odlin showing
intelligence and has got up his home work.

Yr/ *caro collega* E. Miner working on japs?

do you communicate? 849 Stanford Av. Palo Alto.

am returning yr/ carbon, with one line marked.

<*I think H. G. was just tryin to show off that he had read that much Pope.*>

<*Miss Tibbetts uses pen name J. Tibbs*>

                                                    E. P.

27

Aug. 24, '57

Just got back from the hills to find yours of the 13th. I recall the first time I was glad to be a Yank (I stayed British for about 15 years) was aboard the *Queen Mary* where I was invited over to First for "coffee & liqueurs" from Tourist, and was about to dance politely with my hostess' daughter, a millionairess, when several stewards closed in on me with many sycophancies, and this, Sir, and that, Sir, and how the Commodore had said, Sir, that they were not to serve passengers from the tourist class, etc., and it came over me that I had grown accustomed to the peasantry saying, "Get the hell out of here, huh?" . . . . The second was, you might say, last week, since I don't know what other land has taken such elaborate steps to keep such a huge chunk of gorgeous territory for the exclusive possession of the people. My friend Alan Shields (Philosophy Dept.) has become a ranger as of this year. What he didn't know about rocks and all . . . . There too I was much taken, having previously felt the same way as Hogg says about Percy B, when he came stumbling in to their digs from the lecture he cdn't hack after the first ten minutes of it and, asked what it was about, said, "Stones, stones: it was wonderfully tiresome." But now you may ask me anything at all about glaciers, halfdomes, igneous materials, etc. etc.

Who and what is Rock, aside from being Goullart's dedicatee? Did you get the latter thro' Murray? What was it Rock wanted to "answer"??

Isn't it a matter of temperament whether you A) subordinate the 777 jabs to what you DO about it, or B) subordinate what you do to the jab? From the standpoint of my own arrangement of humours, resembled (in this respect alone!) by the *Tao Te Ching*, the A of those two, whilst obviously being more American, is at the same time vulnerable to the useful American cant phrase, "So what?" Actually, I guess neither rates *sans que chacun se répond à l'autre*. If the absolute was going to be construed tomorrow who wd want to wake up? . . .

I am taking liberty of sending under separate cover latest issue, just out, of *Twentieth Century Lit.*, not because of my mayhem on "the Master" (?) but that I thought you wd be interested in their way of getting at what is being said about authors, under *Current Bibliography*, including a couple under POUND. Hope snide piece on James doesn't finish me with you. I only did it because of the way my colleagues all fondle him . . .

Ever get to hear Bernard Paumgartner & Vienna Symph. do Telemann's *Suite in A Minor* for flute & strings? Epic has it with Haydn's D Major ditto on tother side, pretty cherce. Both dedicated to the noble prisoner in the dippydip.

J.T.

P18 / TLS   **28**

J.T.   26 Ag '57

    Rock is the buzzard FIRST heard of Na Khi / 20 years/ bilingual
texts/
        start as botanist, then geog/ 20 years literary
etc. <sunk> by jap torpedo
    in trunk
has answered letters/ no contact with Goullart yet made.
///
am not damning all metaphysical speculation/
St Bernard/ *considerare*. investigate/
          however *con-sidera*
          does it fit stars
Am merely distinguishing 2 *Anschauungs* AND,
                as Confucian, more
interested in what stays SO
        whichever answer yu get to the flummydiddles.
Maverick is yr/ most active bit of Calif/ fauna/ but Hawley also
conversable
JFC Fuller just wrut/ Kuan Tzu top of all econ/ bks he has ever read.
I aint had time fer to listen to discs/
        this to catch post/
    not that yu are in sech frenetic hurry.
Waal when I wuz 2nd. Unc Herbert came down to talk, but then
    I discovered he had done time (I mean I found that out years after)
british civility. ar as Ari sez: not without sufficient cause.

                        EP

Earl Miner, address
849 Stanford Av. Palo Alto

29

8/28/57

Now listen, Magister, who the h is "Unc Herb" (Off hand I only came up
with Herb Hoover, Herb. G. Wells, "Herbie" Read, Bart., & my ole pal
Dave Herb Lawrence; but none of them to my knowledge did time:
besides when wuz EP "2nd" rather than first?) Nothing in context seems to
clear this up: hence JT's IQ falters again. And while we are on civility, and
hell, well that's what with British variety. Only excuse came clear to me
after 3 months in Kono's company: same ethnic, insular defence against
overcrowding (I see Tokyo's population has now gone above N.Y. &
London).

That about Rock cooks me — worse than *French Revolution* being burnt
(too bad Thomas ever bothered to rewrite it) or TeeHee Lawrence (tho' I
never cd quite believe the story about *Pillars*).

I don't believe I ever wd have started my textbook of poetry for the kids
(trying to start them off right) if I'd known what it wd mean. I'm a good
deal crossed up, and the manhours, believe me, are way out of line. I have
to sneak Pound in by the back door, like when in my prefatory preamble,
eliminating deadwood definitions, and I use the following EP as
corrective to the wetyourpantsschoolofcrit (when Housman drools about
"not to transmit thought but transfuse emotions," or some such bosh):
*"thinks, but with what is so imbedded in his nature that it never occurs to
him to question it: not a matter of which idea he holds, but of the depth at
which he holds it."*
(I observe that the syntax of your telegrams was in those days a shade
more ceremonious.)

No metaphysical knockdown-dragout coming up. "Does it fit the stars" is
the payoff as far as I am concerned. Couldn't have been better said unless
you say it. One continues to hope the stars will let on WHY it stays so. Well,
of course, they do.

I don't know why this one is in such a frenetic hurry, except as I say I
absolutely HAVE to know about UNC Herbert.

Afraid I am manic about disks, esp. baroque: partly that I didn't carry
through as practising pianist. I buy them behind my wife's back. I have to
chauffeur her downtown and so I'll mail this before night.

J.T.

P19 / TLS

30

3 Sep '57

or sunk in a sea of suet. Cumulation
of yester inflow.

Let us start concretely, Unc. Herbert. as the TV sez "only the
names have been changed, to protect the innocent."

let us allow the nipots of Unc. H. to enjoy anonymity. you will never have
heard of them or of him save as laboratory specimen, brit. *mores.*

can't isolate components of brain-wash. BUT note the gulph between
J.T. epistolary, and J.T. taykin 'is pen in 'and.

"A Scholarly and critical journal." I take it this is absolootly
the TOP of what the J.S. (Jewnited straits) can DO, *dicto millessimo.*

At least some of you have ganged up and intercommunicate.
aim being to SWALLOW (prophetic name)

That is what you are expected to swallow.
Col/ P…y sends in a very different *Kulturausführung,* wanting my
opinion. Does the name Dilling (Eliz) convey anything
to you?

is there ANY communication between the alarm of E.D. at what is
being swallowed, and the Swallows

cert/ NOT intending to make a summer in
coloRAdo.

what really depresses me is a TEXT BOOK, intended to
feed by pump, as suffragettes etc. in 1913. the YOUNG at initiation
of kawledg career.

H.P. Vincent. Ill. Inst/ Technology, and H.Hayford. Northwestern.
they aim to make the little dears SWALLOW.

BUT, may be there is a gleam? on p. 544.

I was sunk at the appalling
mélange adultère de tout/ the thrusting of the almost good into a
mass of, *vid, supra,* suet.

may be I must dive into this aquarium/
cert/ full of contagions.

How far yu got wiff YOUR tex bk?? I sure wanna see that
as soon as?

if yu prudently make 3 carbons, do yu wanna lend me
the 3rd one?

8.04 a.m.

AN implement, testifying to progress of technocracy now making like
concrete mixer under window/ possibly engaged in pumping bilge out
of basement or whatso??
Ever hear of a bloke named Mayo? (N.western?)

Yr EP

yes, yes, I MEANT to keep track but
damiFI goin to make a cawpy fer file.

P20 / TLS   **31**

J.T.   *5 Sep '57*

Cant be bothered about Henrietta Maria AT this late date

Am sending Zielinsk *Sib*/ to save time/ fer garZACHE get onto
one of the NEEDED blasts.

             the damndest bit of impertinence, cliché,
still SWALLOWED by people as otherwise intelligent as the Agresti.

"Rome giv law, greece awt and the lousy kike give religion."

                  **

I got me nekk out far enuf / BUT all yr/decent orient friends

hinDOO Chino bullawayo etc. ought to DAMN and BLAST and debunk
that sewage all day and every day.

even Plarr's wife's old ld ladies used to amuse V.P. by sayin "he is
not so high as the BhouddHAH!!"

Lust fer luxury, they cen't stand JE-tzu lying in a mere lane and
had to provide a posh manger/

all respectable greek females got fucked by Jove or Neptune
for 2000 years before the patent was swiped in JEWdea.

          to hell/ and to Mel with Hellville/

time for Thoreau revival, not on his Rousseau but on his
perception of better mythology.

go TO it, grampaw can't do ALL the work.

Aint I got a youthful indiscretion still in print somewhere: Fer sheer
dreariness one reads H.J.

     BUT god damn it when they offer William instead of Henry / and
Shapiro before Eliot, and Faulkner before old Ford.

                it is time to look to the stalls
in Augean garage.

             benediction and DAMN

                                     EP

Eliot gits sore
when I speak of his
lousy religion and THEN

bleats that it
"inchludtes the
chewvisch reeLigion"
Evr hear of a gal named Dilling?
Calvin, Cauvin, Cohen, sez Liz. useful item. ever see Wychliffe's
phiz? too bad she needs 22 pages to spill it.

32

Sept. 7

1390 Merritt

To Pound's of 3rd & 5th, my birthday, whether 34th or 74th depending on digestion, arthritis, visible marks of corruption in the body politic, and other vicissitudes. How can I identify what belongs to the specimen if his behavior isn't tagged, as well as innocence protected by change of names.

No; I *said*. I don't give a tinker's cuss about H.J. Just got bored by my colleagues' sycophancy. Certainly I read your earlier thing. You had read your subject, unlike me, except that one they said was the best (*Golden Bowl*). I did like some earlier *International Episodes*. Tried (without) to get thro' *Ambassadors*. Your admiration made perfect sense. Remember Henrietta Maria's specifically assigned reason for absconding with the knives and forks of New England, home & beauty? Our *"parochialism,"* he called it. I can't help thinking the old boy wd fix a grave eye on the frequently profanely announced animus of the most powerful mind of the ensuing generation of scribblers against, "with all its faults," the best protection we have against said parochialism, *viz.*, said "kikes". Some angel in authority ought to prod you to knock it off. I have been sick unto death in Iowa City, the rats, (not metaphorical) coming out of the wainscotting to look me over at 3 and 4 and 5 o'clock, the city (if you cd call it that) surrounded, and if it hadn't been for a Jew there and if it hadn't been for another in Kingston, Ontario, where it was yet more cold, Stephen Wynburne, Irish Jew, second only to you in romance languages . . . I wd *then* (not now) have given up. They are volatile. They can box, act, play the fiddle. I know all they say about them and the sheckels and then some. It's historical. We are entitled to our fire and brimstone, you especially. For my own I will take Sonnet 66: "Tired with all these . . . etc." Right down the line, neither adding nor taking away (much).

And another thing, while I am galling the maestro's kibe. Why pick on Swallow, I mean instead of being grateful for small mercies? He' a good egg, trying to do something. I recall the time I visited Frieda Lawrence in Taos. She was very nice to me, tho' the old lady had had too many tuft hunters down there: Greta Garbo, for XT's sake, and Auden, and H. Miller (who behaves all right except, I gather, for his parasites that he was unable to send packing) and Tennessee Williams, with his boyfriend, trying to get copy (she said, "Zeez boys, I sink zey die off dis ting some time"). After she had described in some detail the late's death, the difficulty she had experienced in believing him departed till it sank in, etc., etc., she said in the vile Richtofen inflections, "He lay dere and I said, dere iss a man who neffer wance compromised." She then gave me the leonine glare and proceeded to enquire of me whether I felt able to match this *nonpareil* of truancy. And this in its turn irritated the hell out of me, and I pointed out to her what I should now like to point out again: "If you are the happy or unhappy owner of a large river of talent, it is a real pleasure when something doesn't sit, to pick up and go to Australia or Italy or gaol. But if you have nothing but a narrow rill, by God, you compromise. And come to that, you compromise when you eat, dress, defecate, and . . ." But frank as she likes to be, I did not feel able to fill in all the other activities incident to drawing breath. End of anecdotage of the "epistolary jt."

James Stephens *mit Frau* will arrive any day now. I guess we'll get him fixed up for a while, tho' as I told him, in my view he shd keep on going to Santa Barbara, if it is knowledge he is looking for. He cd put my knowledge in his eye and see no less, as my mother used to say.

                                                     As ever, J.T.

I hope you are not making me a present of Shapiro and Faulkner, since I am unable to read either one.

It wd be disingenuous to conceal from thee that I shall probably take every precaution to keep the textbook out of your hands before and after publication. —I have become *far* more interested in the Jap poems, corrected proofs of which have reached me. It's now a question of finding the right publisher for the right selection of these, in the U.S., since I feel they have done enough to what they took from Rimbaud to make it a real bonanza.

P21 / TLS   **33**

8 Sep '57

Has J.T.

any information re/ Harrison (Haywire) Hayford and H.P. Vincent
who putt out a tex book fer the lead-and mis- of freshmen

READER AND WRITER/

could be USEFUL/ are there any better ones *in circulation*??

It has decent stuff in it.

Scudder on Agassiz
Hayakawa, a bit of Browning, a bit of Hazlitt.

and a nawful lot of crap/ butter and eggs flowing after brit/
suburbia/ and the N.Yukk weakly slopliments.

Dave been collecting or trying to collect old school readers/
I think there wuz a series of 5.

The stink of brainwash / I shd/ think first lie to BUST,
I mean in any program to clean up the Rooso
Dex White/ etc. sewage is the lie that the kike gave the
world religion.

DISGUST with skunks like Churchill / degeneration
in From old Jerome, simple hearted sport , old Jenny re/
low status of writing, Winston , and Randolph selling
the old sow-face idea of betraying Mihaelovitch.

connect ALL psychiatry with Beria program.

and get a census of russo kike origin of employees .

BUT of course some chewsz ought to be read/ like Rosanov, Montaigne
and Spinoza for their racial symptoms.

RIGHT older than man, to choose own associates. NOW <being> wiped out
by Ike Mr Chavvitt'z man.

<Javitts   Chavez   Tutt   V. Vanti>
ought to be philosophic angle on that.

I cant read any more ABOUT H.J. but the Swedenborg element
IF he got <enuf> from his ole pa H. Sr. could be useful.

E. P.

P22 / TLS

34

Dear Theob/ 11 Sep.

> Yu an the gt/ Mariannah and even O.R.A. marVElous for overlooking historic facts when they don't fit yr/ pattern.

and erecting exceptions into laws.

the PRINCIPLE of DEGRADATION
> of bastardization and *mélange.*

it is good that hindoos be MORE hindoo / that chinks be MORE chink each rising to its own height and not a *mélange adultère de tout.*

and how the hell can I medicate the horrible plague of american university corruption if I dont SEE specimens of what is actually used in the jewricula.

Haywire and Vincent have done a useful job/ so burried in slosh that I doubt if one freshman in 100000 will see the structure unless some

> gift of GAWD to their instructor
> > dissociate the pewk

from the punkins.

How can M.S. get HER text book across unless someone sees what can be putt over, and where the permitted limit is drawn.

I wd/ like (speaking of positive constructions and not Robt. Mond) to know what ten poemS J.T. thinks no freshman shd/ be without.

> I am KOlecting. so far I think the only nomination that has had TWO votes is Mat Arnold *Dover Bitch.* (pardon me, spell it wiff a *ea mi* Ludd.)

I wonder how many of the specific facts I have spent 50 years in collecting are admitted in yr/ cosmos (or Marianne's or her parson brother's).

Tseng has just resigned from Tunghai/ disagreeing with Mission Board/

> I spose Cauvinite money lenders brandishing the cross (of gold or zinc)

AND if I recall the *Gowden Bowl* is NOT on my list of H.J.'s
> productions, i.e. as reading matter.

Fred Manning (*Scenes & Portraits*, 1910) if yu are old enuf for
name to convey anything toyu.
      after all I did write the *Yittischer Charleston Band/*
and tamed the kikitrist in the hell hole therewith.

     (DAMN, started on the wrong line) continue from
anyhow F.M. held that having seen divine vision was extenuating
    circumstance

Beria's brainwash, filth of Vienna / shd/ have been pre-spotted with
exclusion of grammar and freshman COMPosition, substituted by
cWeative wYting.

go back to drive AGAINST gK and latin by 1900 / RECOGNIZED in France
as a POLITICAL issue/
            debated in chamber of deps/ to puzzlement of
yank newspaper correspondents.

/ present enquiry / does or has ANY American prof mention or
mentioned or KNOW of ANY member of his OWN local kawlg faculty who
has any intelligence, and with whom he converses re ANY
serious subject.

ON the spot, Confucianly. I am "issuing" this challenge personally
to my few acquaints IN official POsitions.

If my temporary voluntary sekkertary hadn't alas just been
    ABsorbed
into/ educ/ system, I wd/ git yu a copy of the Agresti's <*aetat 83*> last
letter.

    She done gt/ chapter on Lubin, for future *Edg/*
<another> the ole <*Mish*> gal who started Virgilian Soc/ and I think dug
    masses
of ms/ in forgotten and/or private libraries in Abruzzi
has been edged out by some dam Jesuit/ and
            lofty aim (with unfortunate title)
in process of being verbitched.

J.T. got any idea how to harness "Poetry Societies" to
improvement of text books?

and thereby to fancy-freeER-ing even his own
anagogic velleities??

Incidentally "TIME" is damnLieing again. I did NOT say Hem is
dishonest.

I may have said Spanish reds <were> are phoney, Lice's paper
apparently dont know difference between wop weekly and daily *Il Tempo*.
And I think it was not even in the turk's article, but a sub head
putt in by make-up in Roma.

My longsuffering consort sez I so OFTEN leave out the POINT.

wot I mean IZ: I am ready to examine text books, but damn if I read
the amateur buzzards on your list of the gang you avoid or the
27 other similar congeries slobbeling along at that level

either in metre or *senza*. 5 beat or simple chop.

or uncontrolled kepp'n me kepp'n.

(which can rock an roll.)

ef yew thumP IT

E. P.

35

Dear E.P.   Sept. 15/57

. . .

Stephens arrived, was *bien plus gentil que vous avez dit, pas de tout* "un *idiot,*" *pace* Pound *(comme il n'a jamais voulu dire). Il vous adore* and one has only to utter the names of your detractors to set him muttering expletives. He painted your perquisites, décor and all, with a narrow harrowing palette but hugs hope in that congressman, forget his name.

My textbook has Homer, Theocritus, Ovid, Chaucer, Shakespeare, Blake, Whitman. It also has a great mess of crap and I have no wish to be bullied about what doesn't lie in the scope of my choice. Of the ten best poems you assign me to name, it contains parts of 4: "Prologue," "Hero & Leander," "Venus & Adonis," "The Ecstacie," "Holy Sonnets," "Prelude," "Songs of Innocence & Experience" (Coleridge entirely right about the single best lyric in the English language being "The Little Black Boy":

> *For we are put on earth a little space*
> *That we may learn to bear the beams of love . . .*

Summat of *Leaves of Grass* (I'll find it if I have to), socalled "Grief Sonnets" of Hopkins, for whom personally I feel little but the strongest distaste, *The Winding Stair* poems, and what I am up to hacking from the "canters."

O yes, you asked about Mayo. Assuming it is B.L. Mayo, I thought it rang some bells. He taught at Amherst long after I left there, does presumably operate out of Minn . . . . *My* (it really is that) bk of translations has arrived from Japan. I don't know what to think. It comes out as co-authored by Kono & a character called Fukada, who, according to Kono, took part in 11 out of the 300 poems, all 11 of which had to be mauled by me. There is a brief sentence of acknowledgement to me and "Mason Ingram," a nice guy here in San Diego who once called up Kono on Christmas Eve, San Diego to Tokyo, who never looked at anything in the book and would not know a poem from a pork chop. They do things strangely over there. It is standard, for instance, for an old established man of letters to bring out as his own a translation of an English novel by an unknown youngster like Kono . . . .

J.T.

During these months, Theobald's spirited, gossipy letters on "life" and things literary seemed to provide the right stimulus. Pound's replies came thick and fast and form, taken together, a sort of update, or appendix, to ABC of Reading—certainly a rare enough exercise for him in those years. We see him pouncing with glee on (non-) candidates for his and Miss Spann's anthology; there are to be no cute, no cosy, no soft-headed poems in his anthology (no Herrick); no sunday-school pieties either (no "Dover Bitches" or "little Lambs")—"too bloody much Xtism in the lot uvum," he growls at Theobald: "pre-Zielinski"—and closes, magisterially, "It is asking WHAT can the occident putt up against Kung's Florilegium" (Book of Odes, i.e. "POETRY having contents.")

P23 / TLS

36

YESSA   17 Sep '57
>My esteemed J.T.

>>>THAT is why the Nips were less esteemed in the
tripartito.

>>Or as Ito sd/ to Yamanaka: "I nebr hear we hab any jews in
J'pan. I think yu jap'nese jew."

>*Non son tutti usignoli,* they are NOT alluVum samurai.
The draper in Rapallo said his *confrère* in Sta Margherita was
buying the Porto Fino lace patterns from Japan and selling at ½
the price the local fishwives got for making 'em <*300 years tradition*>
before the japnese competition.

But then Chennevière printed one of Flint's without acknowledgement,
and as e.e.c. remarks: *La Canaille liTTTeraire!!*

no! my Mayo is Robert

>>>AND the Junior Anth/ is 186 pages or
under 6000 lines, so there will be VERY few tax-paying-at-present
writers in company with Homer, Cavalcanti etc.

AND there will be NO long poems save possibly one Crabbe. and
snippets from Homer and Ovid only.

It aint a slumming expedition.

>Am horrified at reopening Chapman. And howling for something
better.

Vince sez Rouse is the best/ BUT there OUGHT to be few bits of
metrical rendering.

Trying to git some fotostats of Ogilby
>to see if key meaning have come thru AT ALL.

The filthy gap between Golding and Gavin D/ and the debasers of
>>Homer !!!! ynnGGh.

How do I git a cawpy of yr/ japn'z??

Yr/ metaphysics seem O.K. ideogramic inclusivity. But
>>>wot am I spected to do about it?

Guy named Merchant, come to Folger

sez they got traductions.

Bion, F.Fawkes, 1760
Theoc. printed for Stephens. 1684

Dont seem to have found the *Sixe Idyllia*. Barnes Oxford 1588.

Is it fair in compiling a seed catalog <&then luring> kids to look at buzzards who have done ONLY the one or two items fit to putt in a anthology.

Having associated with greeks and chinks for 25 years/ an AWFUL shock to try to find more Herrick than "One night in the Year."

300 pages saying: "please copulate"/ in kittenish language.

>Waller, Rose, and Lawes who DID make it.

and then what?

Maverick sends on Williamson: Wang An-shih, with some
>POETRY having contents.

6000 lines, dont give space for Plologue, and Hero, etc.

I dont want snippets save necessarily for Homer and Ovid. Golding serving for the latter. O.K.

>and the HELL to find ANY Homer.

My enquiry/ and my inability to READ stuff in gobbledegook AFTER chink, greek, Fordie, Hardy, etc.

>with DECENT writing in Golding and
the buzzard from Stratford.

>IT comes as a SHOCK to reopen 'em.

at any rate there was no thought of including ten or eleven of the damn bores you mention as such.

I wish Mavrogordato wd/ do some Homer.

Shx/ lyrics so DAMN much better than others.
Joyce never cd/ stomach Browning.

and: "Little Yamm who made thee?

>Bnhaaaa, Gawd he done it!"

too bloody much Xtism in the lot uvum. pre-Zielinski.

only 3 kike religions made religion a *casus belli*.

the LIE in face of China and India/ Je-tzu etc.

Glad you like Stephens.

it is asking: WHAT can the occident putt up against Kung's
>Florilegium??

Giot/ and Bot in painting. O.K.

As fer the U.S. pre 1900
Barbara Frietchie? and wot elsz??

ever see Bayard Taylor's
Faust? did he git it??

E.P.

37

For Ezra Pound: Sept. 18 '57

P. S. Timidities restrained me from this postscript, as perhaps they still
should. Naturally it was damned depressing to read in *Time* about the man
in the iron mask; but you should know that, even as things are, your voice
could be muffled only by your own choice, and not effectively even then.
You continually deplore this trend and that. Meanwhile, any periodical of
note would be elated to print your printable opinions on most of these
matters. The so-called "Little Magazines," some of which are still
comparatively big, would have their tongues hanging out for what you
think of the current crop of verse writers; whilst as for the *soi-disant* big
ones, I don't know why the hell *Esquire* would devote a large part of an
issue to warmed over irreverences about you and not be interested in what
you have to say, altho' honesty and impudence compel me to admit I wd
walk further and pay more for your opinions on what is happening in Lit
than for your fulminations on fiscal betrayals. I fail to see how this
situation can be much altered either by the prolongation of your infernal
incarceration or by your release. What do you mean "muffled"? Our
Upper Division course in Contemp. American Lit. (taught by a young man
called Lee Gerlach, who is an Ivor Winters neophyte and so, presumably,
wd have small *a priori* reason to love you) will take you up and put the
class through a close study of the early poems and first ten cantos.
(Incidentally, I believe Gerlach is quite fond of your son, who confided in
Gerlach that he wd have liked to go after Chinese and Japanese only he
figured "the old man" already had it wrapped up.)

Just received enclosed from the nice sounding Maverick. After some
paralysing hilarity over the kick in the tail, I was duly chastened but
reminded of one of my favorite classroom parables on Art versus
Propaganda. It comes in H.G. Wells' *Experiment in Autobiography* (his
best book) where he recounts the episode of himself and Conrad on the
"bich" and Conrad, pointing out to sea, asked Wells how he wd describe
the movement of a certain small boat on the water. Wells promptly blew a
fuse and started popping off about how he figured himself for about 15
years more to live (he fooled himself there considerable) and he should be
wasting his time describing the movement of a damned boat while the
world was going to rot, etc., et. From which it is a short step to enquire of
the class how many will be reading Wells' various squirmings about the
damn state of the damned world when *Heart of D*, the *Cantos* and other

useless works (for as you know I don't take much stock in the argument about Bulganin leaping and turning pale over the economic impact of Pound) are still being elucidated to wide-eyed frosh. The argument is, of course, old hat—Henry James having set Wells straight about it fifty years ago. I am myself such an infamous goldbrick I am scarcely the one to disparage the interest in time; but I can observe already certain hopeful signs that it's only a question of time before the bloody amulets we carry on the wrist will be found only in museums and such.

As ever,
John Theobald

P24 / TL
38

J.T.   *<20 Sept.>*

THAT, mon cher, is the trouble wiff yu Mahabharattz

Never cd/ tell whether Ghose was burbling re/ this a.m. or something
in time of Kalidasa.

alzo RELATION of dogma to particulars/

          yu git a idea re/ goldbug/
and don't know why the s.o.b. take up Benton when they hear him
called "Old Bullion"

      and drop him like hell's hot iron when they
find out WHY, WHEN, in what circs/

       he wanted metal money.

AND the pretense that the literary shit *<of a >* Niebuhr shunning
exact use of words. etc.

       is all part and parcel of indefinite MIDDLE/
<even> the gt/ Lubin fooling the Agresti/ wanting fixed price
in variable currency.

      And taking NO adequate precaution against tyranny
and melting all men into one stinking pattern.

Yes. Maverick *is* the liveliest mind in this sloppy continent.

AND yr/ naiveté, you being over 30 in supposing that any of Luce, Lice or
Spewlitzer or ANY of 'em want to print the truth.

is a loolahhh.

They want inteviewers. like the perfidious Gun in "*Tempo*"/ who
print part of it and destroy the rest/

      and the copy desk then inserts a
lie not even in Gun's text.

      And as Giovannini notes with fury,
Time then prints the worst.

// one drropp of Comfort. Having requested one of the voters fer
Dover Bitch to read the poem/ which I was bored by 30 years ago
and never reread, and *ergo* was not *in situ* to gauge yr/ and Chatel's
disgust with/

      ebbé, it is discovered that there are 5 lines at the
start/

after which it slobbers/ and the voter, on reperusal
sez NONE of Mat/ A. is fit to reprint.
>   *i.e.* nowt save those 5 lines, and may be
some phrase elsewhere.
What are yr/ views on Bret Harte, Sill, B. Taylor's *Faust*??
It wdn't matter WHAT Wells wrote about/ it wd/ be slop/
>   and not advocating SLOP re/ Royal prerogative or
anything else.
A welchman eating on Folger is looking at Coke, and LAW in
Shakespear.
>   so far have not discovered he hass a chewisch vife or
@ least one rabbi among his ancestors
>   <like the last two engleshmen @ that trough>
Hang onto the Cohen, Cauvin, Calvin, slant and as yu
still vote fer Mark Hanna,
>   occupy yrself with *meta ta phusikaaaa*
and excrete mesopotamia.
H.J. got round to MENEY before he croaked. If he hadn't had
brights disease, hermann's disease, bullowayo's disease/ <etc>
I might have got MORE into his nutt
The hush in his voice when D.P. and H.J.'s niece loped along ten paces to
fore of us in Cheyne Walk, and he recd/ news of alliance.
"is she . . . ah . . . is she . . . ah . . . A
>   COM . . . . . . patrioT?"

H.J. on ANYthing is of interest. H.G. Wells uninteresting
even on sex/ tho possibly immortal on politics in one
phrase:
>   "And leave that old BITCH
>   sitting up there on that
monument."
but that <!> was for the *Sagetrieb*, in the spoken NOT in H.G.'s
merchandize.
>   Whereas Bennett did write stuff he couldn't GET PRINTED,
even while getting 50 quid <regular> fer a narticle in the *Evening Slanderd*.

None of yr/ alledged periodicals ask for AN ARTICLE BY me.
they want me interviewed by trained slops.

39

Dear EP...　　　　　　　　　　　　　　　　　　　21 Sept.

Keats probably felt the same way about Chapman as I, *aetat* 15, felt about Bayard Taylor's *Faust*. I remember the smell of the field in Hassocks where it went in. One isn't fussy about these things till later. For example, I remember a year later being utterly transported by a translation of *Wilhelm Meister* by the most hideous mind that ever disfigured lichuchu, Thos. Carlyle. Keats wd have ended doing the *Iliad* himself with pointers caught from Dante, having already shed as he said "the Miltonic sublime." Rouse's *Odyssey* is a kick, Aircraftsman Shaw style only better. I don't suppose I cd reread any Wells, unless "The Country of the Blind." Odd that he grandpappied such a vigorous, if usually corny genre as "s.f.," — not counting the way they say Polyphemus was science fiction and the cave drawings surrealist and Poe or somebody less likely wrote Sherlock Holmes . . . .

You wouldn't care to lay a modest bet that the *Atlantic Monthly* would print almost anything of yours on the literary scene in the fifties? If you consent to put any ammunition in my hands *re* the interview of this Gun, I will take it up with *Time*.

I am going to have to stall with the Jap proofs. As I said, the book is in hand, but I have sent this to an American publisher, with the idea of cleaning it up (in several senses) and bringing it out over here. I do also have the loose proofs but will be using them in my 149 course. I will, however, shoot it along directly I can. Alas, an awful lot of it is sort of Verlaine-lapsed-in-time-and-passion, but where they stay closest to Basho and Taikan's screens they are ok (I think).

Cohen is as Cohen does. Calvin is the nastiest bastard of them all. Who the hell is Cauvin?

D.P.? D.P.? (I'll probably wake up in the middle of the night with it)

　　　　　　　　　　　　　　　　　　　As ever,
　　　　　　　　　　　　　　　　　　　J.T.

P.S.
Will you consent to settle a bit of literary gossip for us, which always sounded to me like skulduggery?—Joyce purportedly telling Yeats that Yeats was too old for him Joyce to help him. Joyce is not in any case my dish, but I wd like to get him off the hook on that one.

P25 / TL   **40**

24 Sep/befo-brek 57

matutinal rage re/ pp/ in one of yrs, rage increased at bother of not
being able to find, <the passage> possibly back several letters/

re my THINKING I am suppressed/ and that the s.o.b.s wd/ have
tongues out to print what I think re/ writers of today.

It is not the Yale-kike trying to interest me in Talmud/

it does imply getting OFF my own job, and paddling thru a lot of
twiddlers/

      The UNPrintable part of my writing is what deals with
ANYthing of importance.

         I am NOT going to read sewing circle verse
I wd/ be interested in KILLING the dope in text books/

  two interesting (pathologicly) specimens, recently borrowed
from victim who will have to teach "from" them.

neither wholly bad/ do YOU with yr/ gweater ugspurrience
accede to a grope towards categories:

A____ one full of vulgar tosh, possibly sucking up to reviewers
        in hope of benefice, publicity, lift up stairs/

B____ tother DEAD as hell / half century of critical action ignored/
        No Landor, no Beddoes, doubt if there was any Thoreau.

early english o.k. (I spose they had three buzzards, and divided
chronologicly, and the up-to-chaucer bloke guided by Skeat's ang-sax
reader.

      <the others> probably still in the 1888 LOOK to england snobism.

        * * *

Edg/ 7 arruv, you will git yrs/ by surface in a couple of months,
WHEN yu do, mebbe yu wd/ say whether it wd/ be SAFE to divulge
name of virtuous prof/ mentioned as an ameliorator.

Wot I am fumbling at is: I jus' ain' goin to READ a lot of
      village pyanists/

         BUT if there is ANY place to focus criticism
in way to IMPROVE what gets PAST the copy desks AND **gets printed**
in text books, soz NOT to pizon the young,

         lead me to it/

criticism DEFINITELY leading to PRINT.

Alzo/ Vince against obscuring the texts by commentary
       probably NOT against brief historic introds/ telling the
frosh of circs in which, i.e. historic backgrounds etc.

Alzo/ by five beat/ do you mean ti TUM ti TUM ti Tum ti TUM

astrologicly predicting depression, aHHH / *tu ne quaesaris.*

are you old enuf to remember the two frogs/ Phila/ and ChiKago?

looking for an awareness to: what gives/ and coherence and
desire to CONNECT

T16 / TLS

41

Dear E.P.:

Oct. 1, '57

I always envy the people with a lot of nervous energy who don't get migraines after lecturing 3 hrs in a row in competition with the jack hammers installing accessories in the big new Nabisco bldg they've moved us into. Also the people who know how to say go-to-hell when neophytes, Stephens included, land on you late at night with conversational designs, etc.

I wrote you a big tirade consisting of certain chosen lines of Chaucer, Sh'sp & Donne turned into not titum titum titum titum titum, but swung on that and becoming ("with Man, proud man, dressed in a little brief authority," say)

> *tumtiti tumti tum titumtiti*
> *tum tumtiti titum titum titum*
> *titumtitumti tititumtitum*
> *tumtumtitumtitum titum tutumti*
> *titum titum titum etc, etc.*

Twas clear you would not read this guff.

I have a theory about you which ought to be good for at least an article in *Twentieth Century Lit,* except that it will not be writ. The million pentameters in solution in your system blent with the quantitative measures ditto to yield a new sort of counterpoint. For all ordinary purposes, however, if the thing from which you vary is itself a variation, only an ear like yours could achieve recognizable rhythm in English. Hence, Pound's attack on *"rhythmic swat"* was really to rescue rhythmic swat. But you put your big stick in the paws of who knows what sorcerers' apprentices still wet behind the ears, and who will be surprised when they raise the devil with the wrong paw and get dismembered, including Bunting, tho' I grant he is not defunct-trying-not-to-be-moribund, like some of them. Not to mention the alsorans that piss on us in yr name. As when not was an innovator invoked to sanctify every species of s-t, p-s & corruption . . .

J.T.

P26 / TL   **42**

J.T.   4 Oc/ '57

AYE, NOBL BLAST.
        pity it cant be rubbed into H. Louce's moog and rubbed into
Barney's *Egeria*, etc.

I will keep till someone can thermobake or copy. As it is unlikely that
slime will rectify, have you any snobjections to its being,
after due interval, used in *Edg*/ as sample of what Louce and co
do NOT rectify.

obViously, the ten to twenty year job was to git OUT of Browningese
and the *ti* TUM *ti* Tum.

I don't see why all construction on dactyllic hexam or ang/sax
allit/
        or Landor's speculation re/ wot Ovid did in Gaetic as
take off
                shd/ be regarded as rectification OF something else.

esp/ as Shx Jacques runs up to 17 syllables/

and there WAS a wop who divided Dant's eleven into three (ef
I reColect KOrektly or that wuz my himpression).

Grape vine sez *Esquire* going to print some rectifica in nex issue.

I think it wd/ be distinctly useful to putt yr/ goon squad
onto continuing the noise in that quarter. Birmingham evidently
benevolent, tho no longer edtr. etc.

Thanks for swat at Slime.

as to jaKKammerz/ there wuz a buzz on tree machine saw
accompanying my last evangelical discourse to company on way
to Washington (state)
        N.H.P(earson) replies with generalities NOT with *nome. cog/ ed indirizzi*
when asked IF mind at Yale.

JT does not add to mailing list/ let us say 3 names worth postage
of items such as HEREWITH enc/d.

gt chapter from O. Rossetti Agresti memoirs, re Lubin, just sent to *Edg.*
along with Dudek broadcast.

In these letters (one from Theobald, to which Pound's peppery and resilient letter of Oct. 17 is clearly a reply, is missing), Theobald touches pluckily on several sensitive points—Roosevelt, Keynes, Hemingway, et al. Pound's responses are sharp and immediate, a succession of large and small explosions, with characteristic abrupt dicta (e.g. apropos of Benjamin Whorf's new Language, Thought and Reality which Theobald had been urging on him, "can't letch after things with kathol. titles"). He defends "Hemingway's timing," possibly in reference to the latter's 1956 remark, "Ezra should be released from St. Elizabeths and allowed to practise poetry without let or hindrance" (Look Magazine, Sept. 4); or perhaps to Hemingway's, Eliot's and MacLeish's more recent efforts to get the Attorney General's Office to, at long last, drop the treason charge. True to form, Pound quickly converts mere acerbity into an educational opportunity: Keynes is succinctly deflated; Theobald is urged to read Otto Eisenschemmel on the circumstances surrounding Lincoln's death; question is raised as to the degree of freedom manifested by Eliot's metric vis à vis Beddoes' (does Eliot seem to "limp" by contrast?—c.f. Canto LXXX: "Curious, is it not, that Mr. Eliot/has not given more time to Mr. Beddoes . . ."); he insists on the indispensability of Coke's Institutes and Blackstone's Commentaries to a proper curriculum ("Shd/be required for ANY bachelor's degree/") and stresses again the importance of Linnaeus and Agassiz, as well as Benton and Van Buren ("to find out what manhood could be" on this "degraded continent").

Certain names, Coke, Blackstone, Benton, Van Buren, Agassiz, Linnaeus, form an ideogrammic cluster in the present correspondence and elsewhere in the later work of Pound. It is not an arbitrary grouping. What they have in common, and mutually reinforce, is in fact that first article of the Imagist creed from years before, "direct treatment of the 'thing' whether subjective or objective," i.e., having the eye uninterruptedly on the object, not on one's thoughts or feelings about the object. It is the kind of objectivity he had admired in Corbière, who "looked the thing in the eye and was no more minded . . . to soothe the world or the world-of-letters with flattery than he would have been to deceive himself about the state of the channel off his native village." Except for Linnaeus, each of the above has had a fair amount of notice in Pound studies. His comments (Feb. 4 '57) "pt/of Linnaeus is that he wd/teach ORDER in composition," and "gt/poet C.L." (Carolus Linnaeus), certainly invite a closer look at him, as does Marcella Booth's remark: "The kind of poetry he wanted required infinite care. It would take months, he said, for his study of Linnaeus to improve his use of adjectives. He spent them."

(Paideuma, vol. III, no. 3, p. 334.)

The great *Swede's* Systema Naturae, his Species Plantarum, and the record of his Lapland explorations, all exhibit certain habits of style and procedure, in addition to those mentioned by Pound, that are of interest to the student of the Cantos. He is a master of capsule descriptions of natural objects. He loathes blurred or imprecise terminologies, redundancies, needless classifications. He is terse, laconic, elliptical, often (notebook fashion) omitting verbs or other parts of speech when they are not essential to meaning. He is "ching-ming" incarnate—taking, in fact as one of his maxims, these words from Isadorus: "If you know not the names, the knowledge of things too is wasted" (Critica Botanica, p. 1). Like Pound he teems with almost tyrannical, common-sense pronouncements: "If a generic name is suitable, it is not allowable to change it, even for another which is more fitting," and "New generic names are not to be coined so long as suitable synonyms are available" (90-91). There are also, here and there, touches of dry Poundian drollery: "Locality often makes plants a little different, but it has never changed one species into another, not even in the brain of any sane botanist (130)." (cf. "oak leaf never plane leaf"—Canto LXXXVII.)

P27 / TLS

43

Dear J.T.   17 Oct/57

     you are FAIRLY wet. Refusing to see Roosevelt as a cad, and
a liar who perjured himself every time he took oath of office.

Refusing to note the nature of the fight/ from 1919/; FROM the
betrayal of the U.S. in 1913/; from the total history

assassination of Lincoln etc/ AND the people who dared not
buck the great infamies, or who merely said that THEY hadn't
the power to fight.

                Hem's timing has been excellent. The
LIES of the burocracy and the acceptance of them by several
celebrated individuals who might have declined to accept 'em.

The worm Page (Giorgio) <*no connection with* **Paige**> gave away part
of the show/

Have you spent half an hour on either Law or the
Constitution?

JT try kindergarten course re/ biographies of Beria, Dex-White,
Perkins, Hopkins.

Do you think I am the ONLY opponent of shittery who has been
"bugged"??

qt/ from <*correspondent in*> western bughouse: 7. Oct. '57:

"After asking if I thought the Fed. Res. was bad, the psychiatrists here
decided to give me a combination of insulin and electric shock
treatments."

In short you attribute to "my friends" an inventiveness, which
does not, to the best of my belief and information, accord with
chronology.

The statistics of russian immigration and the number of immigrant
     kikiatrists now
drawing pay from the boobarican taxpayer??

                      Dont stifle yr/ curiosity.

Even Maverick hasn't answered my last questionnaire, but
has divagated onto prince-indices.

Lubin wanted farm prices stabilized (IN an unstable medium of
eggsChange controlled by the Kikeshields of Rot.)

glad Stephens not being a bore (or not too so)

Small sample of Whorf wd/ be welcome but all LICHERRAY
endeavors shd go to STOCK,

if he falls fer 'em, it is o.k.
with me.

Ryozo sent me the Japthology / he is NOT in it / evidently
??a cleaner gang is in opposition, tho the Junzaburo is shown.
How much of it <the others> do YOU think worth printing?

I've not been through it, gave it to Sheri M to
éplucher.

Never DID like it rosé/. BUT there is excellent peruvian
or whatever Reisling. or is it Chile?

You might note the correspondence in Esquire current issue. Friend and
foe/

the quality of the opposition/ the charrming etc.

also the curious mendacities which the professingly
benevolent Gun gets into Tempo, Aug 29/ and the
different lies in the Schweizer Illustrierte Ag 26/

a much better blurb BUT gratuitous lies.

the flights of fantasy??

A Jap English studies/ special Wm Blake issue Oct 1.

claims to be vol CV <no, vol. CIII>, no 10

know anything re Kenkyusha Pub. Co.?

EP

44

Oct. 21, '57

ok, ok, *domine*, don't be disdainful just because I pass along what seemed to have some of the earmarks of evidence. If they had compounded to get me impounded by distorting my visible excitabilities to fit their bloody psychoses, I trust I wouldn't give them the satisfaction of fitting it all into my political prepossessions, rather than pinning it down. The huge boil of E. Hemingway's ego would *not*, in my opinion, ever make him not a straight shooter — if only because not to shoot straight wd hurt said ego more than anything else could! . . . Let it go: I sound to myself more and more like Iago. There certainly never was any idea that friends did not act out of notions of love and rescue, however much these ideas may have gone sour in the upshot.

I don't seem to have very much curiosity to stifle about either economics or germ warfare. Fiscal fiasco in one disguise or another always seems to revert to the Marxian hypothesis, which is nothing but envy of creative comfort. I have read some Keynes, Parrington, Julian Huxley on the viruses and the international exchange; and the argument that both of them affect me and the human race intimately has about as intimate an effect on my mind, apparently, as the argument (quite valid, I am sure) that inter-service rivalry is certain to result in the liquidation of the city of San Diego. Going somewhat further afield, Jefferson is to me an old-time statesman whose surviving writings make less interesting reading than either Burke on the one hand, or Rousseau on the other. (Eliot's dislike of the latter, derived from the awful Irving Babbitt — what an appalling ass he was —truculent old SOB too — made me admire Rousseau all the more, a good musician in several senses.) Lincoln? Why *was* he assassinated? He was, as politicians go, better than average; and I have never confessed to anyone until this moment, not even myself, that I always felt Whitman's adulation to be faintly ludicrous . . . Living in the c 20 demands a strategy of partition: that which is admirable, that which is interesting, that which is boring, and that which is beneath notice. I shall not provide any more specific examples of the four kinds, having already got into enough trouble with you for one letter.

The dead young Whorf, as far as I know, is owned by the TECHNOLOGY PRESS OF MIT (his *alma mater*). True, Hayakawa's *"etc."* got hold of his essay "Language, Mind, and Reality" (1941) and printed it for the first time about five years ago. Terrific event to all who got to it. It knocked me for a loop. Then — *Nothing* till the *Language, Thought and Reality* book in 1956 (Libr. of Congress Card Number 56-5367) which I have only just found. Whorf himself, who looked like one of my students — I mean almost any one —gave the credit to Sapir and, even more, Fabre d'Olivet. Ha! Like Fielding ascribing himself to *Gil Blas*. Sure it wd be marvellous if Stock would print, say, "A linguistic consideration of thinking in primitive communities" lying around in *ms* since 1936!!!), tho' it sometimes sounds as tho' his big things, like the Zielinsky, interest him for his own not necessarily so big *ad hoc* reasons. I could not introduce Whorf. Not a philologist, let alone linguist. Whorf was on his way to mastering all known tongues and coming up with the clue to the lot, and what's more, to them as the clue.

Read your treatment of poor Housman's "Name and Nature of Poetry" to my class. Much laughter and applause. He was one of the unhappier fairies, like Butler — tho' naturally I did not mention this fact. I always liked Yeats' remark: "A mile further and all had been marsh." I know nothing of Ryozo or a rival gang. How do you mean *Junzaburo*? Believe I told you Kono had eaten crow. What a letter! I believed it all. I believe practically everything that's told me (except things about your imprisonment).

As ever, J. T.

Thanks for mentioning the Blake issue. I never heard of Kenkyusha, but there is a lot going on over there. They'll be making a move to translate you if they haven't. Good God, Kono has just done *Other Voices Other Rooms!*

P28 / TLS

45

J.T.   <*24 or something Oct.*>

    IF you *will* read a slop like Keynes/ and think economics is
the brainwash and slosh advertised by the kike press and the
Churchiloian sewer/

      OB

      viously it aint worth yr/ time

    Keynes to C.H.D.: high cost of living due to lakk of LAYBBouhr.
2 million out of work in London at the time.

                      la meRRRDRE.

    Glad of direct impression of Babbitt/ whom I have never separated
from Sinc. Lewis' character/

      in TOTAL ig/ and incuriosity re/ both.
You are fairly cheerful, but think how much MORE so, IF you
had spent more time on good books and less time on drivvle.

Linc/ assassinated fer having understood wot Jef/ wrut to Crawford in
1816.

    Eisenschemmel, worth reading on known circs/ in the sense of
immediately surrounding details and s.o.b.

Damn all/ TRY it and whatever on Stock, I don't back seat drive him.
But he ain' got *froid aux yeux.* If he dont TRY <*to*> print it it *will*
be cause it borEZ zim.

Recd/ Yr/ Oxford Odyssey from Miles Payne/ with a letter he wd/ not
have written if he had READ any of my writing.

    especially any pages of same tending to keep meaning of
words

    DISTINCT and not messing one with another.

Can yu convey to to the sd/ Pain in the ??

or to Stephens, the need <*of*> looking at the printed page before
asking for personal attention.

there is also the Dantescan line/

    che il giudeo fra voi di voi non ride.

    If Stephens wants to educate his ?? landlord ?? let him try to.

Disappointed because I expected the letter/ encd/ with the vol/
to be from you.

and meant to peruse with care before dwelling
further on yr/ brief epizl of the 20 onct inst.

The NAIVE Meacham eggzorts me to make soothing statement in the
PRESS/

suggesting some of the slimiest corners/
and OBlivious that
for one fact put over, the stink of hell will print several
more falsehoods.

AND that from 1913 the attempt of journalism to
get ANY decent writer to waste time on choinulists
is a consuete
disc.

I am evidently indebted to the Payne in the q/
for the vol/

but will not try to fit yr/ psychoses to anything until I have
had leisure for perusal and meditation.

Scarfoglio had been ten years on bk/ of search from common origin
of languages

when I last saw him/ which was in woptalia.
He has done some of my Kung Odes into wop/

and hope he will do the
lot.

Might circumvent Harvard sabotage and get the seal text
printed via Roma.

K.L. Beaudoin mentions Yu Suwa
another of the 3000 not in yr/ NipThology.
and a muggerzoon "Kast"

wot iz MIT?

wot HEKASTA does Whorf drag in?

I cant letch after things with
kathol / titles.

Ryozo Iwasaki done vurry hansome biLingual Mauberley, and
some buzzard done *How to read.* Junzaburo is in yr/ KonoThol
p. 102 did introd to Ryozo's tr/ at least I think he did. Very hard
to keep 'em sePARate.

eggskewz disjointed etc.
      <for the sake of promptitude>

an' about that tumpty tum question/ When did you last look at
Beddoes?

        Don't he answer quite a lot?

The Eliotic <limp> has had 40 years instead of 20
                    is it a lasting life-line?

T'row out deh . . . .

If by any chance you do think of looking at T.L.B. let me know
before hand cause I been looking fer a <particular remembered> line
      and haven't found it.

and the next peruzer might/

                                        27 Oc/ E.P.

P29 / TLS

46

Dear J.T.   *31 Oc/*

      Congrats on NOT having wasted time on Keynes/
and <tis> no news that God-Damn-Hell Cole as he wuz known to Stella
and Phyllis is unreadable, having seen his semi-animate carcass I never
tried.

      C.H.D(ouglas), soc. credit movement been goin so long, the
initials known in many parts as well as G.B.S. among stinking fabians.
dry stincgk.

If Pain in the Q/ wants to be useful, let him start getting both Coke and
Blackstone bak in curricula/

                 shd/ be required for ANY bachelor's

degree/

          BOTH for history and for english prose/

Damn it I only got Coke this morning, or yester. I mean G.Giov.
brot 2nd/ *Institutes* yester, and I only got the full sense of
clarity an hour or two ago.

                  DAMN the shysters who have bitched all
education in our jewniversities.

                   the sooner someone wakes up to the fraud
the better.

          DECAY of mind/ J. Adams the TOP, and steady decline
          in quality after Benton/

last gleam 1878 ????

ANYhow if yr teackin eng/ prose LOOK at some Coke or Blackstone, and
lay off the Miltosh and pewkery and etc.

Sandbag wont READ any history/ only sob stuff.

<get> Eisenschemmel, but better read yr/ Benton and VanBuren, to
find out what manhood could be in <this> be-jewed and besmeared
and degraded continent.

yep. Carl is "sorry for" / but I thought he was all out for
Leopold Loeb with greater specific vigour before Lorraine mentioned
me to him, a few weeks ago.

             still he did mildly deplore the kewpie doll

NOT of course capable of clear idea, re/ for example, VERY old right

    long before Maggie Charter: right to choose one's associates.

I hear S. Carolina is emotional.

Cant have ideas re/ Whorf till sombuddy pesters me with the TEXT.
        Ox Od/ manifest of intelligence, but I got to read COKE.

and you know enough to keep you busy without my spending 4 hours
    trying to make an intelligent comment, ANalysis ugh.

answers to rest of yr/ lr/ are in Kung/ *Pivot* and *Analects.*

Y *EP*

47

Nov 4/57

Thanks for the note about Beddoes. The last time I looked at *Death's Jest Book*, I remember thinking that the pentameter resembled *Witch of Atlas*, minus the latter's peculiar airy drift. What did you mean about him? By the way, not meaning to toot or anything like that, but if you glance at St. 40 of Ox.Od., you will note it not only has that 17 syllable line you ascribed to Shaksp., but the *average* count on that 14-line whatdoyoucallit is between 13½ and 14, all pentamic swot, by me. Not that it matters. Since its subject is searchforgawd and that dignitary is invariably lost by being named, I ought to take another shot at it some time, less circumscribed in ostensible action, and freer in movement. Can't seem to spout the stuff and teach, or is this an illusion? . . .

Wish I knew how to get Whorf to you — assuming Libr. of Congress to be unavailable. The book is $7.50 for some reason. Ever hear of a current *philosophe* called Wheelwright? He's no Whorf but has done some thinking on these lines. Also knows *Upanishads*. His best book called *The Burning Fountain*. He lekcherd here and handled himself well. O yes, and what I really wanted to ask you was how and why H.G. Wells ever managed to steal the thunder from Olaf Stapledon (*Last and First Men*)?

Anent yr urgency that I read *and teach* Coke. Again, I cannot think that this represents your considered judgement, or at any rate that it is what you wd advise or practise yourself if you were on the pedagogical firing line. One sees the point of a man of very great resources of expression directing himself and less disciplined authors to the *Civil Code*, as Flaubert did. That was part of a specific stylistic battle (similar to your own versus the gorgeous georgians). For teachers of English, however, De Quincey's dichotomy (the literature-of-knowledge versus lit-of-power thing) has come to have an almost desperate importance. Actually. I think it's a losing game and now with the hue and cry about the incommensurably greater number of engineers in Russia than here, I predict that the Humanities are due to be in full retreat. In this campaign I can assure you that no flank is going to be turned by admonishing the wavering lover of the arts to peruse an English jurist of the turn of the 16th century, unless you count Bacon as such . . . .

As ever, *J.T.*

After a six weeks' interval, Theobald writes again with an account of a
UFO sighting, and his reflections on the event, as well as, surprisingly, the
fairly direct complaint that E. P. is unwilling or unable to interest himself
in any "concept or body of knowledge" not already "part of your stock-in-
trade." Pound's response (Feb. 3) is masterly, full of a dry, undismissive
humor, enshrining a memorable irony—inmate of federal insane asylum
expressing concern for sanity of American public outside—and a jeu
d'esprit worthy of James Joyce: "my pilGRIMage thru the wail of tears."
The opposition of calyx (Linnaeus, minute particulars) and saucer
(indefiniteness, fantasy) is picked up the following day: "pt/of Linnaeus is
that he wd/teach ORDER . . . every term . . . meaning something specific"
in contrast to the current mode of "ANYthin', positively, welcome if it
keeps 'em off basics."

Pound's last letter, ten or so months later, is from Schloss Brunnenburg,
Italy, not apparently in answer to one from Theobald. One is immediately
struck by the altered tone and style—cordial, lucid, quiet, unreminiscent
of the peppery epistles of the St. Elizabeths years. Gone are the vorticist
ellipses, the frisky truncations, the typographic high jinks, the outrageous
puns; instead there are complete sentences, a level narrative tone,
"standard" diction and syntax, and a seeming weariness of mood, or
impulse, incipient perhaps, but pervasive. As the final letter in the whole
series, however, it is exactly and affectingly right; and also quintessentially
"Pound"—including the recognition of new achievement, that familiar
cry for help for somebody (in this case two deserving European scholars)
and the closing request for any reportable "indication of mental life," off
there in California, six thousand miles away.

48

Jan. 26, '58

Jim Stephens always seems to refer to you as "Gramp": an agnomen that wd be most unsuitable as coming from me, if only because of the moments when I experience a semigrandavuncular sensation in your direction.

Since we were last in correspondence with each other, I have myself become interested in the iron hand of American bureaucracy; and it may interest you the more that it was in connection with an incident of a kind that has landed many a better man behind bars in a criminal dippydip. In company with my wife and a friend and about thirty others I had a sighting, clear as gin (but without benefit of alcohol), lasting between 10 and 15 minutes of what has come to be referred to as an U(nidentified) F(oreign) O(bject), before it took off at an unassignable speed into the stars. No known human aircraft behaves at it behaved. So I began to read up, having previously been a, shall we say, reluctant sceptic. Esp. Major Kehoe's *Flying Saucer Conspiracy,* which establishes beyond shadow of doubt that the Pentagon has been for at least three years, and perhaps longer, engaged in a systematic policy of suppression of all relevant information . . . . You probably read how 2 nights ago Kehoe was shut off the air; or maybe you were watching that show, tho' I doubt if you bother with TV, as I do not. I don't completely rule out the possibility that some Krauts got to Peru with the secret of propulsion by utilization of the magnetic field (shutting off gravity: in fact, some of the reports lend a faint color to this notion, tho' I still prefer to allow the wish to father the thought that they are outofthis world). I would put you onto a course of saucer readings, since there's a growing literature, but I incline to the view that no one on this earth can persuade you to read a book that you had not previously resolved to read, or to look closely at a concept or body of knowledge which was not already part of your stock-in-trade. Thus, for example (nothing to do with saucers) there's a terrific exposure of the Amer. setup came out in '56, called *The Power Elite* by C. Wright Mills (Oxf. Univ. Press). But I consider it extremely unlikely that you wd stir a step to procure it, let alone read it. Discouraging.

Want me to write Duncan? Sure. What's the scoop? Is he spozed to have the inside track on sumpn?

Sure was nice to hear from you. Like I say, maybe we'll soon be fellow inmates.

As ever, J.T.

P30 / TLS

49

3 *Feb/58/* dear TIB

        Am not crabbing yr/ bloody saucers/ and
shd/ I say I have never seen a duck-bill'd platipus, I shd/ not
expect you to interpret it as denial of possibility of such an
animal's having hit the optic of some other individual.

Being inclined to Plotinus' or whomso's view that the body is
inside the soul/

        and knowing of NO intelligent tradition <*to effect*> that
there is NO intelligent *ens/* but he and she humans,

        I fail to see why an intelligent entity
floating or leaping or galivanting in space shd/ need to be
"human."

        I can't DO anything about it/ and there has been a
flux of TV phantassy spent on it.

        DISTRACTING possibly some
attention from local and merely human affairs.

        in which a little sapience,
literacy or simple sanity might ameliorate the lives
(if there are to be any) of our offspring.

ne ultra crepidam.

It wd/ have saved me time to have seen copies of Coke and Linnaeus
earlier on my pilGRIMage thru the wail of tears

        or hilarity
(depending on temperament of the pil.)

If you LIKE the present tax system, that is an indication of
taste, personal, and to me somewhat curious.

O.K. saucers difficult to examine/ calyx (botanic) more approachable
        second kindergarten/ proficuous, conceivably for nipots.

Gordon having got to Brunnenburg seems to think he is in *settimo
cielo.*

        E. P.

P31 / TL **50**

4 *feb*/ fergot I hd/ putt sombuddy'elsz' letter into *macchina*.
<*hence abbreviated p. 1*>

the point IS re calyx vs/ saucer.

OUR generation was fed a lousy curriculum/ and it has
steadily decayed since our time.

we had pewk for history, and they now give Tocqueville
and omit Coke.

pt/ of Linnaeus is that he wd/ teach ORDER in composition

and that no one learning language, latin in that case, CD
get bitched with abstractions

every term having an OBJective

relative, that is to say meaning something specific, co/relatives
might come later/

but every damn term means a specific object,
colour, form or zummat.

It is time for us to go to second kindergarten/

incidentally

nobuddy will LEARN anything now from J.J.

nuissance value T.S.E. ?? R.A. reports first edn/"Sweeniad"
5000 sold out/

not that I cd/ read the damn thing or wd/ try
<ANYthin, positively, welcome if it keeps 'em off timely
basics>
but it must indicate some sort of OBjection on part of
shirts stuffed or whatso

fais q' ou' 'ouldra/ discouraging number of bugs invented
since the Sweede started his catelog/

gt/ poet C.L.

yes, I discover the moon, twice in past 12 months. Oke Hay
it is, or is not, funny, Oke hay, it is funny,

and I am perfectly
willing to hear about saucers/ <Col.> Ergot was more vigorous Sunday,
mebbe he dont need HIS retirement

voice of colleague on ward: "driven OUT of one's soul." *Sagetrieb.*

P32 / TLS

51

Dear J.T.

19 Oct 58

My head works very slowly and I have been put off by
hearing that "there is no italian version of the book of the Dead."

I mean I thought the Rachewiltz translation was merely the
italian version of what Budge had already done in english.

Finally seeing the magnificent Scheiwiller proof sheets,
(bilingual) it has penetrated my skull that this is the Turin
ms/ Saitic text, not before done into any language.

AND apparently the Brit. Museum
<photo reprod> reprint of Budge a few years ago, did NOTHING but reproduce
the old edtn/ taking no count of anything learned re/ Egyptology
in the interim.

These two young men are doing on their own what OUGHT
to be done by some large foundation,

IF there are any Foundations using
serious work.

Yale did NOT print Maverick's Kuan Tzu, merely
handled it for a time, etc.

Do you know of any man of good will
in ANY of the organizations who would take an interest in the
quality of work which I assume to be present in this edition?

I dont know that there is anything to be done
now save recognize it, and possibly reward it, if they ever
reward.

Have very little energy, and have never had time to
carry on correspondence interrupted last spring. You might greet
anyone in yr/ ambience who sent congrats/ at that time, and tell
'em to send on any indications of mental life since observed
by them (or even caused by them, if any).

Yr, Ez.P.

Notes & Glossary

Notes

Notes to Introduction

[1] See the lucid exposition of Douglas' ideas in Hugh Kenner's *The Pound Era*.

[2] One of Pound's mentors, Senator Thomas Hart Benton, had made a similar point addressing the U. S. Senate in 1831: the Bank of the United States (affiliate of the Bank of England) "tends to beget and prolong unnecessary wars by furnishing the means of carrying them on without reference to the people."

[3] Pound takes the term "Misprision of Treason" from Sir Edward Coke's classic *Institutes of the Laws of England,* 1628. In *The European,* August, 1957, Pound cites Coke on misprision as follows: "Misprision cometh of the French word *mespris,* which properly signifieth neglect or contempt. . . . In legall understanding it signifieth when one knoweth of any treason or felony and concealeth it, this is misprision, so called, because the knowledge of it is an ill knowledge to him, in respect of the severe punishment for not revealing it . . . [for] he ought with as much speed as conveniently he may to reveal the same. . . ." (pp. 282-83. Editors' ellipses.) Pound's letter to Theobald of 31 Oct./57 would appear to indicate that he read this passage in Coke for the first time on that day; yet he had clearly grasped the principle of "Misprision of Treason" long before that, whatever one thinks of his application of it, for in the Rome broadcast for April 23, 1942, he comments: " . . . any man who submits to Roosevelt's treason to the Republic commits breach of citizen's duty."

[4] Hilda Doolittle. See her *End to Torment.*

[5] In the 1918 essay "Henry James," *Make it New* (New Haven, 1935), p.255.

[6] For an astute discussion of Pound's stylistic techniques, *see* John Steven Childs, "Larvatus Prodeo . . .," *Paideuma,* vol. 9, no. 2 (Fall, 1980), 289-307.

Notes to Letters

1

Sq $ series: Square Dollar Series; *see* Glossary.

Hildebrand: identification not certain at this date. Perhaps ? Joel Hildebrand (1882–1983), distinguished chemist and faculty member of the University of California at Berkeley for 69 years. Officially retired in 1952, but continued to teach graduate students, conduct research and write. Stated: "Brains are not such a drag on the market that they should be deactivated prematurely."

2

Dexter-Weiss-White: Harry Dexter White, (unofficial) assistant Secretary of the Treasury, under Henry Morgenthau, 1941; appointed by Truman executive director of the International Monetary Fund, 1946; was accused of spying for the Soviet Union, 1948. Symbolized for Pound Jewish infiltration of the American government.

Lightfoot: Probably Joseph Barber Lightfoot, Bishop of Durham (1879–89); wrote on the *New Testament*, the Church fathers, and other theological matters. Pound was undoubtedly familiar with his *Clement of Rome* (1869).

Shehan: Fulton John Sheen (1895–1979), Roman Catholic bishop who conducted a popular television series, *Life Is Worth Living*, and was the author of polemical religious best-sellers.

Maritain: Jacques Maritain (1882–1973), Catholic theologian and philosopher. Author of numerous works on philosophy, politics and aesthetics. A main proponent of a neo-Thomist approach to religion.

Libury'em at Ham Coll: Librarian at Hamilton College (as well as Professor of English Literature, Anglo-Saxon and Hebrew), Joseph Darling Ibbotson (1869–1952); *see further* Ezra Pound, *Letters to Ibbotson, 1935–1952* (Orono, ME: National Poetry Foundation, 1979).

Sewing Circle Gazette: Pound's sobriquet for *Poetry* magazine, and, by extension, for all "literary mags."

Chicago office: Poetry's editorial office was (and still is) in Chicago. *Poetry* was edited by Harriet Monroe from its inception in 1912 until her death in 1936.

Carruth: Hayden Carruth served as editor of *Poetry* from May 1949 to January 1950. Under the editorship of Carruth *Poetry* published a pamphlet (1949) defending Pound against Robert Hillyer's attack in the *Saturday Review.*

Neo Thomist Poem: see letter of May 28, 1957.

3

Kung: Confucius.

Blackstone: see Glossary.

P. C. Das: Prafulla Chandra Das; *see* Gallup D198.

oriya: one of the main Sanskrit languages of India.

Krishnamurti: Jiddu Krishnamurti (1895– ?), Indian theosophist; born at Madras, founded the World Order of Star in England with Annie Besant; in 1925, she pronounced him the new messiah (a claim he repudiated in 1928). Author of *The First and Last Freedom* (London, 1954); *Commentaries on Living* (New York, 1956); *Beyond Violence* (New York, 1973); *et al.* Situated in California.

Confucius "Pivot": The Unwobbling Pivot & The Great Digest (New Directions, 1947). Dated "D.T.C., Pisa; 5 October–November, 1945."

Chakravarty: Amiya Chandra Chakravarty (1901–?), Indian author, scholar: *The Dynasts and The Post-War Age in Poetry* (N.Y., London, 1938); *The Indian Testimony* (1953); *Mahatma Gandhi and The Modern World* (1948). Pound dedicated *The Unwobbling Pivot and The Great Digest* to him. [Square Dollar Series, 1947 ?] *See* Gallup A58b.

what Jefferson wrote: see Guide to Kulchur, "Introductory Textbook," Chapter II.

Reid: Ralph Reid (who appeared in *Edge* 5)?; David Reid?; Ben L. Reid?; reference uncertain.

Niebuhr: Reinhold Niebuhr (1892–1971), Protestant theologian; from 1928–60, professor at Union Theological Seminary, New York City. A former pacifist, he supported the U.S.'s entry into World War II; later he had considerable influence in the U.S. State Dept.

Kung: Confucius.

Mencius: see Glossary.

Agassiz: see Glossary.

right place: emphasis on gradations, human and cosmic?

Erigena: Joannes Scotus Erigena (*c.* 810), Irish Neoplatonic philosopher; invited by Emperor Charles II (*c.* 847) to take charge of court school at Paris. Translated works of Pseudo-Dionysius and Maximus the Confessor; author of *De divisione naturae* and *De egressu et regressu animae ad Deum.* Mystical philosopher of a theology of Light and gradations of being as emanations of the divinity, which is the unity of being and mind. His *De divisione naturae* of special interest to Pound in *The Cantos* and elsewhere.

R. St. Victor: Richard of St. Victor (d. 1173), Augustinian theorist of the degrees of spiritual love in the soul's ascent in contemplation of the divine; stressed clarity of perception for meditation. *See* Pound's *Selected Prose, 1909–65,* ed. William Cookson (New York: New Directions, 1973), pp. 71–2. A selection from his writings, translated by S. V. Yankowski, appeared in *Edge* 1.

Cherbury: Herbert of Cherbury (1583–1648), English metaphysician, poet and diplomat; brother of poet George Herbert. Author of *De Veritate* (1624); *De Causis Errorum* (1645); and *Religione Gentilium Errorumque apud Eos Causis* (1663). Contended that truth could be derived from what is universal, and that there exists a natural religion; held that innate truths in the mind give meaning to experience. Maintained that the origins of all religions must first be investigated historically and then be tested by the Common Notions—universals known to all men in all times and places (in 1645 edition of *De Veritate*).

Rémusat: Charles, Comte de Rémusat (1797–1875); French politician, writer on philosophy: Abélard, 2 vols. (1845); St. Anselme de Canterbéry (1854); Lord Hubert de Cherbury (1874).
Pusey house: see Theobald letter of May 24, 1957.
Swabey: see Glossary.

4

gt/betrayal: see letter of June 3, 1957.
Sandbag: Carl Sandburg.
head: Reinhold Niebuhr, Professor of Applied Christianity, Union Theological Seminary.
G. F.: "Goodly Fere."
Faber's collection: Ezra Pound, Selected Poems, edited with an introduction by T. S. Eliot (London: Faber and Faber, 1928). Eliot had remarked: "I omitted 'The Goodly Fere' because it has a much greater popularity than it deserves, and might distract some people from better work of the same period" (p. xxiv).
two chaRRRRming young people: unidentified.
Robert: Robert II Curthose (1054–1134), eldest son of William the Conqueror; Duke of Normandy. Brother of William II Rufus of England who twice attacked Normandy, 1091 and 1094. As an aftermath of the first attack, Robert was forced to cede two counties; as an aftermath of the second, he ceded Normandy to William for money for the First Crusade. When Robert left for the Crusade in 1096, he mortgaged his kingdom to William, who immediately thereafter added Maine to his domain.
Rufus: William II Rufus (1056–1100), youngest son of William the Conqueror; King of England from 1087–1100. Considered a tyrant by his feudal barons; two baronial revolts occurred during his reign—the second put down with brutal force. St. Anselm, archbishop of Canterbury, was forced to flee England due to his opposition to William, who afterwards seized the lands of Canterbury.
Thiers: (Louis-) Adolphe Thiers (1797–1877), French statesman and historian; founder and first president of the Third Republic. Author of Histoire de la révolution française and Histoire du consulat et de l'empire.
Louis X: Louis X, Le Hutin ["The Stubborn"] (1289–1316), Capetian king of France. In order to gather funds for a projected campaign against Flanders, Louis sold charters to nobles and the clergy—whereby certain powers were ceded to the church. Louis also sold serfs their liberty, thereby weakening serfdom.
xt/: Christianity.
enc/: enclosure unidentified.

5

Spectator: Spectator (London), April 26, 1957, p. 542: "Alanbrooke, Pound and British Strategy" by Capt. S. W. Roskill, and "Pound—Another View" by Ludovic Kennedy—both articles concern Admiral Pound.

6

vebbl: venerable?

poEM: Hemingway's "Neo-Thomist Poem" first appeared in *The Exile,* edited by Pound, no. 1 (Spring 1927). There were four issues of this magazine, devoted largely to propagating "a new civilization." Hemingway's note to the poem reads: "The title 'Neo-Thomist Poem' refers to temporary embracing of the church by literary Gents."

Launcelot Andrews: Lancelot Andrewes, Bishop of Winchester (1555–1625); author of a number of religious lectures and devotional treatises, as well as tracts on the relationship between the power of church and state. *See* T. S. Eliot, *For Lancelot Andrewes* (1928).

Tielmann: most probably Telemann.

Radhakrishnan: Sarvepalli Radhakrishnan (1888–1975), Indian philosopher and politician, once president of India (1962–7). Writer on Hinduism and the Vedanta; stressed intuition and contemplation. Author of *Indian Philosophy* (1923–7) which gives an historical account of the Indian tradition of absolute idealism; *The Hindu View of Life* (1926); *An Idealist's View of Life* (1932); and *Eastern Religions and Western Thought* (1939–40).

polite to him in Moscow: Radhakrishnan had been Indian ambassador to the Soviet Union from 1947 to 1952.

compagnevole animale: social being.

Carson Chang: author of *The Development of Neo-Confucian Thought,* 2 vols. (New York: Bookman Associates, 1957).

Baruchistan: i.e., the United States. The word is a play on the name Bernard Baruch (1870–1965), American financier, and government advisor; chairman of the War Industries Board (1918–19); advisor for F. D. Roosevelt's administration and author of *American Industry in the War* (1941); and parodies Baluchistan (Pakistan).

Orage: see Glossary.

Mahabharatt: Mahabharata, Indian epic composed between the 2nd century B.C. and the 2nd century A.D.

The Point: a pamphlet publication, produced by (ex-)Fr. Feeney, which contended that the Catholic Church had been taken over by Jews.

APO: *see* Gallup B58. APO = "A Po[und]," or "Academia Poundiana": "an organization to more clearly define terminologies, and to combat the blackout of history" (E. P.). The APO publication, issued by Vanni Scheiwiller (Milan, 1956), was *De Moribus Brachmanorum,* edited anonymously by Pound. The text is a translation of *De Gentibus Indiae et Bragmanibus* by Palladius (*c.* 430 A.D.) and uncertainly ascribed to St. Ambrose; hence the title page of the edition lists *"falso adscriptus."* Mention of it appears in *Edge* as well.

Louis X, le hutin, of France: see note to letter of May 21, 1957.

7

Blavatskites: followers of Madame Blavatsky, founder of The Theosophical Society and prominent in London 1885–1900; *see* note to letter of June 7, 1957.

G. R. S. *Mead, Quest Society:* George Robert Stow Mead (1863–1933), theosophist and writer on Gnosticism. Collaborated with—as well as being a critical observer of—Madame Blavatsky. Founded the Quest Society (1909) and edited its quarterly review from 1909–30.

Pse•los' refinements: (Pound's Greek rendering for) Michael Psellus (1018–78), Byzantine Platonic philosopher and statesman; initiated a Byzantine renewal of classical learning which later influenced the Italian Renaissance. Served as Byzantine state secretary and headed philosophy faculty of the imperial university. Reformed the university curriculum by emphasizing the Greek classics (esp. Homer). Possessing encyclopaedic knowledge, Psellus composed treatises and poetry—characterized by forceful, and at times virulent, expression—on themes in theology, philosophy, grammar, law, medicine, mathematics, and the natural sciences.

Edge: see Glossary.

F. *Masai:* Pound wrote in a letter (February 3, 1957) to Wyndham Lewis that the Société Guillaume Budé was "started in 1917 to keep greek texts printed with froglation. The LAST citadel of frog decency. . . . F. Masai on Plethon notes that gods are gods cause they got more *hilaritas* than the *animal electoral,* and also that they COMMUNICATE more rapidly with each other" (as quoted in Timothy Materer, "Ez to WynDAMN," *Helix,* 13/14 [Ivanhoe, Australia], p. 156). Masai contributed a letter to *Edge* 6, approving of their publication of Zielinski in *Edge* 2.

soc. G. Budé: Société Guillaume Budé, a classicist organization which still publishes a *Bulletin.* Mention of it appears in *Edge* 5.

Rock: see Glossary.

Goullart: see Glossary.

Krishna M/: Krishnamurti.

Radha /k: Radhakrishnan.

Chak: Chakravarty.

was kept in cage: unidentified; ? was not allowed to reside with his wife due to enforced segregationist policy in South.

La Forgue: Jules Laforgue (1860–87); French symbolist poet, a master of lyrical irony and one of the initiators of *vers libre.* Attracted to Buddhism and German philosophy (Schopenhauer and von Hartmann). His poetry was praised by both Pound ("the dance of the intellect among words") and T. S. Eliot. C. Guenther's "Laforgue and Jammes" appeared in *Edge* 4 and Laforgue's "Pierrot" in *Edge* 8.

8

Ernest Wood's "Digest": Ernest Wood (1883–?), author and translator of works on Indian philosophy and theosophy. Translated *The Bhagavad Gita* explained (section of the *Mahabharata*), etc.

9

Bghsz: "bughouse."

APO: *see* note to letter of May 28, 1957.

G. G.: Prof. Giovanni Giovannini; *see* Glossary.

Migne: Jacques Paul Migne, editor and publisher of an immense library of religious texts, most notably the *Patrologia Latina* in 221 vols. (1844–64).

Possum: T. S. Eliot.

Ford: Ford Madox Ford.

Prufrock: T. S. Eliot's "The Love Song of J. Alfred Prufrock" (1909–11).

Fielding and Miss Tomczyk: Stanislawa Tomczyk (Mrs. Fielding), a Polish medium (fl. 1908–10). Her séances at Paris and Geneva were conducted under experimental test conditions, supervised by Flournoy, along with other parapsychologists; *see Canto* LXXXII.

recent TIME *for phz of Connant:* ? reference to James Bryant Conant, American educator; *see* portrait in *New York Times Magazine* (December 9, 1956), p. 49.

on mediation: on meditation?

John Berry: John Berry (1915–?), author of *Krishna Fluting*, a novel, published by Macmillan & Co., 1959.

"composed of societies": reference to E. Swedenborg's *Heaven and Hell*, VI, *passim:* "The Heavens consist of innumerable societies . . . at a distance from each other as their goods differ . . . [these] societies of Heaven have communication with one another . . . [for] Heaven in its whole complex reflects a single man." Thus, Hugh Kenner's efforts to establish a group at Santa Barbara, and others to do likewise in other parts of the country, were for Pound—to some extent ironically, perhaps, but on the other hand quite seriously—the forming of such societies, among and between which he worked indefatigably to foster and maintain communication.

10

Blavatsky: Helena Petrovna Blavatsky (1831–91). Russian born (co-)founder of The Theosophical Society (1875) for promotion of a Hindu-derived system of religious and philosophical thought; prominent in London 1885–91; author of *The Secret Doctrine, Isis Unveiled, et al.*

11

jecte sa gourme en jeunesse: "sowed (jête) his wild oats in youth." [French]

Dulac: Edmund Dulac (1882–1953), book illustrator and set designer; designed the masks and costumes for W. B. Yeats' play *At the Hawk's Well*.

Iseult: Iseult Gonne, Maud Gonne's adopted daughter, presented by Maud Gonne at first as her niece, but perhaps was her natural daughter by a French politician, Millevoye. After proposing marriage again unsuccessfully in 1917 to Maud Gonne, Yeats in turn proposed to Iseult, who also turned him down.

a friend of H. D.'s: Frances Gregg, a close friend of H. D.'s in 1910; married Louis Wilkinson, a friend of J. C. Powys, in 1912.

Echoes: G. R. S. Mead, *Echoes from the Gnosis* (1907).

Zielinski: see Glossary.

Anselm a sane trinity: "for the supreme spirit conceives of (*intelligit*) its memory as a whole, and loves it, and remembers its love as a whole, and conceives of it as a whole. But we mean by the memory, the Father; by the intelligence, the Son; by the love, the Spirit of both." "Monologium," LIX, in St. Anselm, *Basic Writings* (LaSalle, Illinois, 1974), p. 121. Difficulties in relating the persons of the Trinity and their functions long exercised the early Church, eventually (with the *"filioque"* doctrine of 589) producing a split into the Eastern and the Western Churches. See also *"filioque,"* letter of July 1, 1957.

B. V. M.: Blessed Virgin Mary.

On, Jah: see Edge 2 (Zielinski issue) and *Edge* 5 (Swabey's "Examination of Scotus Erigena").

Gesell: see Glossary.

Elsom: John R. Elsom, author of *Lightning Over the Treasury Building; or, An Exposé of Our Banking and Currency Monstrosity—America's Most Reprehensible and Un-American Racket* (Boston: Meador Publishing Co., 1941).

Sandbag's Lincoln: Abraham Lincoln; The Prairie Years and The War Years (New York: Harcourt Brace, 1954) by Carl Sandburg. *The War Years* originally published in 1939 (hence Pound's remark on "reissue" of *"ianiania"* in letter of August 3, 1957).

Scharmel, Iris: Iris Scharmel (1889–?), remembered for volume of poems, *Bread out of Stone* (Chicago: Regnery, 1943), preface by W. B. Yeats and epilogue by Oliver St. John Gogarty.

Honest Abe who got shoot: see also Colin K. MacDonald, "Why Was Lincoln Shot?" *Edge* 6 (June 1957), pp. 19–20.

Chatel: John Chatel, a young disciple of Pound's who was a frequent visitor to St. Elizabeths; contributed "Bouvard: Flaubert on Money" to *Edge* 5 and "Note on Portugal" to *Edge* 7.

Cavour: Count Camillo Benso Cavour (1810–61), Italian statesman largely responsible for uniting Italy under the House of Savoy; served as first prime minister of new kingdom. Founded newspaper *Il Risorgimento.* Served as minister of agriculture; wrote on financial and political matters.

Chao: Tze-Chiang Chao, Chinese scholar of the *Kuan Tzu* of Kuan Chung and translator of Tu Fu (some of which appeared in *Edge* 1).

Tu Fu: Tu Fu (712–70), Chinese poet; standard biography: *Tu Fu, China's Greatest Poet* by William Hung (1952).

Kuan Chung: see letter by Pound of July 10, 1957 where he refers to "the Kuan (Chung) Tzu," and Glossary.

Harvard delay: Harvard University Press was preparing to publish Pound's translation of *The Confucian Odes.*

Brunton: Paul Brunton (1898–?), author of *A Search in Secret India* (Dutton, 1935), which purports to give "the truth behind the legends . . . concerning- . . . yogis . . . and faqueers."

Petrie: W. M. Flinders Petrie (1853–1942), archaeologist and Egyptologist. Contributed to the techniques of field excavation and invented a sequence dating method. Founder of the Egyptian Research Account (1894) [later known as the British School of Archaeology]. Author of *Methods and Aims of Archaeology* (1904) and *The Formation of the Alphabet* (1912).

Kingsland: William Kingsland, early 20th century theosophist; author of *The Gnosis, or Ancient Wisdom in the Christian Scriptures,* etc.

Miss Tseng's bro/: reference to brother of Pao Swen Tseng; both were still living descendents of Confucius. Miss Tseng had visited Pound in Rapallo in 1928.

S/: Sheri Martinelli?; Swabey?

portagoose trans/: see Gallup D209.

Wang: David Wang, a Chinese-American graduate of Dartmouth and member of Pound's St. Elizabeths circle; involved in translating Chinese texts; mentioned in the later *Cantos.* Selections from his translations of Tang and Sung poems appeared in *Edge 3.*

Loré: Loré Marianne Lenberg, German scholar from Freiburg; part of her Ph.D. dissertation ("The Coherence of the Pisan Cantos") was done under Hugh Kenner at Santa Barbara, 1957–8.

"Child of Vaterland": cf. Henry James, ". . . the deep-lunged children of the fatherland" (quoted by Pound in "Henry James," *Literary Essays,* ed. T. S. Eliot [New York: New Directions, 1954], p. 297). *See* Pound's letter of August 3, 1957.

A.B.: i.e., A.B. degree; reference is to Wang, four lines above.

their 2nd ranking versifier: unidentified.

USIS: United States Information Service.

12

Upanishads: Hinduism's thirteen basic metaphysical-religious texts.

Mahabharata: Indian epic composed between the 2nd century B.C. and the 2nd century A.D.

Kamasutra: Hindu manual on the art of love-making.

"Jodindranath's occupation": "Jodindranath Mawhwor's Occupation," a satiric story, or sketch, by Pound parodying aspects of Hindu "cult" voluptuousness, especially the *Kamasutra,* as well as by implication Rabindranath Tagore. First

published in *Pavannes and Divisions* (New York, 1918).

Jos Pijoan: i.e., José Pijoan y Soteras (1881–?), author of *History of Art*, trans. Ralph L. Roys (New York, London, 1927), *University of Knowledge*, vol. 1 (1938) and *Art in Ancient Times* (Chicago, 1940). *Edge* 6 states: "Joseph Pijoan has a good page on art of the Far East, in one of those curious collections aimed at the spread of culture [*University of Knowledge*], which the U.S. produces from time to time . . ." (p. 30).

Glenn Frank: Glenn Frank (1887–1940), editor-in-chief, *University of Knowledge* (Chicago, 1938–   ).

Santiniketan: "abode of peace"; Rabindrinath Tagore's school at Santiniketan, near Bolpur, India, 93 miles from Calcutta, founded in 1901; here he sought to blend the best of Eastern and Western religious traditions.

Tagorism: Rabindranath Tagore, 1861–1941, Bengali poet, dramatist, mystic; awarded Nobel Prize for literature 1913; acquaintance of Pound and W. B. Yeats in London in the early part of this century.

Kuan Chung: see letter by Pound of July 10, 1957, and Glossary (*Kuan Tzu*).

Santayana: George Santayana (1863–1952), American philosopher and humanist; taught at Harvard University; lived in Rome from 1921 until his death. Author of: *The Sense of Beauty* (1896); *The Life of Reason* (1905–6); *Realms of Being* (1928), and the novel *The Last Puritan* (1935).

Swed/: Swedenborg.

Marano angle: ? reference to a marano (or marrano), a name applied in medieval Spain to a Christianized Jew or Moor, especially to one who merely professed conversion to escape persecution; hence, a forced convert; ? reference to Fosco Maraini, art historian, especially of Japanese art, who had been involved with Radio Roma.

Florence Farr: Florence Farr (1860–1917), British actress, friend of Yeats; she gave frequent public recitations of his poetry; member with Yeats, of central committee of the Order of the Golden Dawn; in 1912 went to Ceylon to become principal of a Vedantist seminary for girls.

woptaly: i.e., Italy.

Blavat/: Mme. Blavatsky.

Eusapia Paladino: Eusapia Paladino (1854–1918), celebrated Italian medium and "magician."

aggiornare: "bring up to date."

Current: leaflet edited by Paul Koch at Cape Cod, Mass.; publisher of Four Winds Press.

Moribus Brachmanorum: see note to letter of May 28, 1957 regarding St. Ambrose.

13

Academia Bulletin: leaflet edited by David Gordon, a frequent visitor to St. Elizabeths.

Uberti: Naval capt. (ret.), Ubaldo degli Uberti (1881–1945); chief of the Navy Press office in Rome; friend of Pound from 1934; translated (into Italian) a few pieces by Pound on fascism, and the opening of Canto XLI; mentioned in Cantos LXXVII, LXXVIII, LXXXIX, XCV (see "History of a Friendship," Italian Quarterly, XVI [Spring, 1973], 95–107).

[Read's] latest collection of essays: The Nature of Literature, by Herbert Read (New York, 1956). The remark quoted by Theobald (on "revolution begun by Wordsworth") is from chapter 8, "Poetic Diction," p. 48.

Hulme: T(homas) E(rnest) Hulme (1883–1917), Bergsonian and anti-romantic British writer on philosophy and literary theory, 1911–14; associated with the Imagist movement, though not its founder as sometimes held. Killed in World War I. See Pound's "This Hulme Business" (reprinted in H. Kenner's The Poetry of Ezra Pound, 307–09); and Canto XVI, l. 119; LXXVIII, l. 70.

Li-Ki: Chinese Book of Rites; 1st century B.C. repository of Confucian thought, ritual and ceremony. Translated by James Legge (1885) in "The Sacred Books of the East" series (Li Chi).

that caste: harijans.

14

Hulme's notes pubd/1927: Notes on Language and Style by T. E. Hulme, ed. Herbert Read (London, 1927). Read also edited Hulme's Speculations (London, 1936).

Herbie's racket: Herbert Read was Hulme's principal editor and literary advocate.

DEEP ones to Ford: See in particular Pound's "Ford Madox (Hueffer) Ford: Obit," Nineteenth Century and After, August 1939, 178–81. Reprinted in Selected Prose, 1909–65, ed. William Cookson (New York: New Directions, 1973). See also the Ezra Pound/Ford Madox Ford correspondence: Pound/Ford (New York: New Directions, 1982).

Ron Duncan's Mag/: The Townsman: A Quarterly Review (London, 1938–82), ed. Ronald Duncan, British poet, friend of Ezra Pound. Pound's note "This Hulme Business" appears in the January 1938 issue; reprinted in H. Kenner, The Poetry of Ezra Pound (New Directions, 1951), pp. 307–09.

Harry Kemp: Harry Hibbert Kemp (1883–1960), minor American poet and playwright: The Cry of Youth (New York, 1914), The Passing God; Songs for Lovers (New York, 1919), et al.

WOLLER TOOT: voilà tout (French): "that's all."

phoney anarchy for parlour use: Pound refers to Read's Poetry and Anarchism (London, 1938), or his later Philosophy of Anarchism (London, 1944). Both are genteel essays rather than objective studies.

Possum: T. S. Eliot.

Nieb/: Reinhold Niebuhr.

King Bolo: "King Bolo and his Big Black Kween." Obscene ballad by T. S. Eliot. See reference in Vortex, Pound, Eliot and Lewis by Timothy Materer (Cornell,

1979), p. 27.

Alan Watts: Theobald had referred to Alan Watts, writer on Zen Buddhism, etc. Pound refers to Harold W. Watts, *Ezra Pound and The Cantos* (Chicago, 1952).

Ciardi: the poet and translator, John Ciardi.

W. Watt: reference uncertain.

Kung-thology: Pound's translation of the Odes of Confucius: *The Classic Anthology Defined by Confucius* (Harvard University Press, 1954).

Arnaut Daniel: Twelfth century Provençal troubadour. "The culture of Provence finds perhaps its finest expression in the works of Arnaut Daniel," Pound wrote in *The Spirit of Romance* (New York: New Directions, 1953), p. 39.

boys in S. Paolo: the *Noigandres* group: Augusto and Haroldo de Campos, Decio Pignatari and Goulart Nogueira; Pound's Portuguese publishers, in São Paulo: *Canteres* (1940), a bilingual version of several *Cantos* and some fragments. *See* Gallup D209.

going on from Mallarmé and Rimb/: *Edge* 6 writes: "Concentrating the heritage of Mallarmé's extreme phase and of Rimbaud's sonnet on the vowels, attention to the word in all its components and phases has never been carried so far as by this Brazilian group" (p. 30).

B. Baruch: Bernard Baruch (1870–1965), American financier and government advisor; made fortune in stock market speculation before 30; chairman of War Industries Board (1918–19) and author of *American Industry in the War* (1941).

Winchell: Walter Winchell (1897–1972), American journalist and commentator for *New York Daily Mirror,* and over radio.

Javitz: Senator Jacob Javits (NY-R) called for "an investigation by the House Administration Committee . . . of the Library of Congress for award of Bollingen prize to Ezra Pound (under indictment as fascist traitor) . . . the dangers of fascism are just as great as that of communism and need just as much examination." (*Congressional Record,* Aug. 2, 1949, p. 9924).

Bubblegum award: The first Bollingen prize for poetry was awarded to Ezra Pound in February, 1949, for *The Pisan Cantos.* This provoked a bitter controversy— which amused Pound—over the propriety of giving such a prize to a person under indictment for treason.

Div. Com.: Dante's *The Divine Comedy.*

Shx Hizzeries: Shakespeare's Histories.

Charlie: Charles I of England, beheaded in 1649 after trial by Parliament.

Shx demise: see Canto CVII, ll. 51–2.

Current: see note to letter of June 12, 1957.

down you: i.e., don't you.

beanerOcracies: i.e., universities.

Gen. del Valle: see "An Open Letter" by General Del Valle which appeared in *Task Force,* no. 2. *See also Canto* CV.

Adm. Beatty: David, 1st Earl Beatty (1871–1936), commanded Britain's first battle cruiser squadron in the Battle of Jutland (1916); 1st Sea-Lord, 1919–27.

Jale: Yale University Press.

Andrew D. White: Andrew Dickson White (1832–1918), U.S. minister to Russia (1892–94) under President McKinley; wrote *Autobiography* in 2 vols. (New York, 1905). From 1868–85, he had been President of Cornell University, where he battled to establish a "common sense curriculum." White's down-to-earth approach to whatever he undertook would make him an attractive figure to Pound. (*See* letter to Swabey of July 1, 1957.)

Bob McA/: Robert McAlmon, American poet, short story writer and publisher; friend of Pound and Joyce in Paris in the twenties. Founded Contact Publishing Co. in 1922; works by H. D., W. C. Williams, Hemingway, G. Stein, etc. were issued by Contact Editions. Contributed to Ford's *Transatlantic Review* and *The Exile* (no. 2, 4). *See* R. McAlmon and Kay Boyle, *Being Geniuses Together, 1920–30* (London, 1970; reissued by North Point Press, 1984).

amurka: i.e., America.

Friedman: ? Lee Max Friedman (1871–?), writer on problems of American Jewry: *Early American Jews* (Cambridge, 1934); *Jewish Pioneers and Patriots* (Philadelphia, New York, 1943); *et al.*

KAHAL SYSTEM: "Kahal," an autonomous Jewish community, within but separate and distinct from the non-Jewish population. During the 19th century in Russia, the Kahals were deprived of all but spiritual jurisdiction, and eventually compelled to assimilate or emigrate.

Hroosia: i.e., Russia.

Protocols: Protocols of the Elders of Zion; documents (now presumed forged) purporting to be the outline of a plan of international Jewry for world domination. First appeared in a St. Petersburg newspaper in 1903 and then published in book form in 1905; subsequently republished in several languages in many editions.

C. H. D.: Clifford Hugh Douglas.

Morgenthau: Henry Morgenthau, Jr. (1856–1946), Secretary of United States Treasury, 1934–45.

sent me . . . : page mutilated and last part of sentence is missing.

15

New Reflections . . . : "New Reflections on The Golden Bowl," by John Theobald, in *Twentieth Century Literature,* ed. Alan Swallow (Apr. 1957–Jan. 1958), vol. III, pp. 20–6.

Hudson: William Henry Hudson (1841–1922), British novelist and naturalist; *Green Mansions* (1914), *et al. See* E. Pound, "Hudson: Poet Strayed into Science," *Selected Prose, 1909–65,* ed. W. Cookson (New York: New Directions, 1973). Hudson was a favorite stylist of both Ford and Pound.

Auden: W. H. Auden.

16

Anschauung: "outlook," "perception," "view" (*German*).

Vendramin: Palazzo Vendramin, on Campiello della Chiesa, Venice. (*Cf. Canto* LXXVI, 1. 265.) Richard Wagner resided for a time in the Palazzo Vendramin, and died there on February 13, 1883.

Gertie: Gertrude Stein (1874–1946); American writer: *Three Lives* (1910), *The Making of Americans* (1925), *et al.* Along with her brother, Leo, gathered an outstanding collection of modern painting (including works by Picasso, Cézanne and Matisse).

Amy: Amy Lowell (1874–1925); American poet, critic; associated *c.* 1913–14 with Imagist movement, which she fostered; dubbed by Pound "Amygism."

city of Dioce: Pound's visionary city of justice and order, toward the establishment of which all positive human effort is directed. (*Cf. Canto* LXXIV, 1. 11.)

PAIdeuma: Pound's term for "the tangle or complex of the inrooted ideas of any period," "the gristly roots of ideas that are in action." Pound took this term from Leo Frobenius's *The Origin of African Civilizations* (1897–8).

y.m.: young man.

d.g.: David Gordon, visitor of Pound's during the St. Elizabeths years, specializing in Chinese and Confucian materials; translator of Chinese poetry. Edited in Washington, D.C. the leaflet *Academia Bulletin;* secretary of the Academia Poundiana. His "Mencius" appeared in *Edge* 1 and his selection from Igor Stravinsky's *The Poetics of Music* appeared in *Edge* 7. Editorial assistant for early volumes of *Paideuma* and frequent contributor.

the Keppertl: capital.

this parenthesis: Pound is responding to Theobald's query of June 21 re the existence of any effort "to establish that if Pound is nuts I am Bishop Sheen." Pound characteristically deflects the emphasis from himself ("sob stuff") to the larger public issue—the U.S. government's violation of a citizen's right to due process (suspension of *habeas corpus*). But, he adds, "*if* sob stuff re/ME can lead to any clarity in civic thought, go on and SOB."

hab/corpus: habeas corpus. Cf. The American Constitution, sec. g(7): "The privilege of the writ of *habeas corpus* shall not be suspended, unless when in cases of rebellion or invasion the public safety may require it."

concitoyens: amalgam for "fellow citizens."

Roman correspondent: Vanni Teodorani, Consigliere Communali di Roma.

dallo scontro dogmatico, siamo già alla crisi pragmatista: "from a conflict over principles, we have already arrived at a real crisis."

beloved daughter: Mary de Rachewiltz.

consiglio communale: Communal Council of Rome.

treccie bionde: blonde tresses.

toilet: i.e., toilette (special attire: false face, etc.). The allusion is ironic, collating double stance of Pontius Pilate, double sense of Saul/Paul, false wigs of English and Irish judges, and "sob stuff re/ME" as highlighting basic issues—violation of a citizen's "legal and constitutional" rights.

17

that compendium on you: probably *An Examination of Ezra Pound, A Collection of Essays,* ed. by Peter Russell (New Directions, 1950), containing eighteen essays by T. S. Eliot, W. Lewis, M. McLuhan, H. Kenner, E. Hemingway, *et al.*

St. Ambrose arrived from the Digger: ? The Diggers (fl. 1649–50), a group of English agrarian communists who contended that the English Civil War was fought against both the king and the large landowners, and that land should be made available for the poor to cultivate communally; the relation with St. Ambrose (Bishop of Milan 374–97) is unclear.

18

Swb/: H. Swabey. Copy of letter from Pound to Swabey (July 1) enclosed in letter (July 2) to Theobald. *See* Glossary.

Fowler: Thomas Fowler (1832–1904), British author: *The Principles of Morals* (1886–7); *Progressive Morality* (1884); *The History of Corpus Christi College* (1893).

Mommsen: Theodore Mommsen (1817–1903), German historian and archeologist: *The History of Rome,* 5 vols., trans. W. P. Dickson (New York, 1900); *Histoire de la Monnaie Romaine* (Paris, 1865–75); *et al.*

Grotius: Hugo Grotius (Huig van Groot, 1583–1645), Dutch jurist; *De jure belli et pacis* (1625), *et al.* Grotius' work has been fundamental to the theory and practice of international law.

Mensdorff: Count Albert von Mensdorff-Pouilly-Dietrichstein; agent in Europe for the Carnegie Endowment for Peace; Pound and Mensdorff sent letter to Executive Committee on causes of war (1928). Letter reprinted in E. Pound, *Impact,* ed. Noel Stock (Chicago: Henry Regnery Co., 1960). (*See* Stock, *Life of Ezra Pound,* p. 276.)

Nic Smeary Butler: Nicholas Murray Butler (1862–1947), political figure; president, Columbia University (1901–45); president, Carnegie Endowment for International Peace (1925–45).

Mary: Mary de Rachewiltz, Pound's daughter.

stews/: "stewdenks," i.e., students.

y.v.t.: yours very truly.

Fatty Can: Vatican.

cat/g/: category.

Bankhaus Pacelli: see *Canto* C: "Durch das Bankhaus Pacelli kompromittiert."

Groot: see Grotius.

Bülow: Bernhard Wilhelm von Bülow (1885–1930), nephew of Prince von Bülow (Prussian statesman); served as head of the League of Nations department in the Prussian government from 1923.

Converge/ or vtx last week: "Convergence or vortex [of items, or communications] last week"—which Pound proceeds to touch on.

Agresti: see Glossary.

Agresti/rehabilitating Augustine: cf. article *"Per il xvi centenario di Sant' Agostino."*

R. R.: Ralph Reid extracted a selection from F. L. Wright's *Future of Architecture* entitled "Organic" for *Edge 7.* Pound is listing, rapid fire, the authors of articles, etc. that deluged him "last week."

Lao Tze: Lao Tze (c. 604–531 B.C.); presumed founder of ancient Taoism, religion of mystical contemplation, knowledge of the "way." *See Cantos* LIV, LV, LVI, LVII, LX, LXI.

Stock/: Noel Stock, editor during the St. Elizabeths years of *Edge,* and of the Australian literary quarterly *Meanjin;* author of *Poet in Exile: Ezra Pound* (Manchester, New York, 1964) and *The Life of Ezra Pound* (New York, 1970). Once Pound's disciple, his recent writings have been rather critical of him (*cf. Reading the Cantos*).

Albertus de la Magna: Albertus Magnus (1206–80), scholastic philosopher, with wide and accurate knowledge of physical sciences of his time. (Hence Pound's reference pre-Agassiz.) Article on Albertus Magnus appeared in *Edge 7.*

Charles Martell: a student in 1957 at St. Lawrence University; published in the college literary magazine (*The Laurentian*) short articles on Pound and essays from *The Exile.*

H. Comfort: Howard Comfort (1904–?), taught Latin at Haverford College; author of *Studies in Byzantine Land-Leases* (Haverford, 1939).

one of few books: Andrew Dickson White's *Autobiography.*

Tolstoi's muddle: see especially vol. II of Andrew White's *Autobiography,* pp. 72–100, for record of White's meeting with Tolstoy; includes his observations on Tolstoy's religious beliefs, alms-giving, etc.

filioque: The early Christian Church had differentiated the relations of the Son and the Holy Spirit to the Father by affirming that the Son is begotten by the Father, but the Holy Spirit proceeds from the Father. The question arose as to whether the Holy Spirit might proceed also from the Son. In 589, the Council of Toledo ruled that the Spirit proceeds also from the Son ("*filioque*"); but this doctrine has never been acceptable to the Eastern Church.

Koine ennoia: "common sense" (Greek).

C. H. D.: C. H. Douglas.

hic est medium mundi: "this is the *way* of the world" seems Pound's meaning here in this letter, in contrast to "center" (*cf. Canto* LXXXVII, l. 156).

White's vol./ on War of science vs. theology: A History of the Warfare of Science with Theology in Christendom by Andrew D. White (New York, 1955, reprint of 1895). In vol. II (p. 267), White claims that St. Anselm "proved from the Scriptures that the taking of interest is a breach of the Ten Commandments," which links Anselm with Pound's views on usury.

Atreides: see Aeschylus' *Oresteia.*

Boris: (Prince) Boris de Rachewiltz, Pound's son-in-law; archeologist and Egyptologist; specialist in Middle-Eastern and African cultures, and translator of Frobenius into Italian. His translations from Egyptian into Italian formed the basis of Pound's *Love Poems of Ancient Egypt.*

Spurt of Romance: E. Pound, *The Spirit of Romance* (New York: New Directions, 1953). See especially pp. 99, 156–7.

19

Hem: Ernest Hemingway.

MacLeish: Archibald Macleish (1892–1982), American poet, playwright, critic; Librarian of Congress, 1939–44; Assistant Secretary of State, 1944–5. Took a prominent part in the movement to obtain Pound's release.

Possum . . . has signed recent evangelical: T. S. Eliot had been very active in attempts to secure Pound's release from St. Elizabeths.

Gugg "Gregory": Gregg Gregory. (Apparently) the prominent British financial pundit and writer on socio-economics: honorary Fellow of The London School of Economics, 1958.

Bible Bill in Alberta: William Aberhart (1878–1943), Premier of Alberta, 1935–43; advocated Social Credit, though unable to implement it very successfully; founder of the Calgary Prophetic Bible Institute.

Bankhead: John Hollis Bankhead, II, U.S. Senator from Alabama, 1931–46. Pound recalls his conversations with Senator Bankhead in Washington in 1939 in *Canto* LXXXIV, ll. 6–9.

Ac. Bul.: Academia Bulletin, a Pound-instigated publication of St. Elizabeths years, edited by David Gordon. *See Paideuma,* vol. 3, no. 3.

Dante vs/ Temporal Powers: context suggests Dante, like Shakespeare, was distinctly suspicious of (opposed to) unregulated secular authority.

A. D. White: Andrew Dixon White.

Chas/ lost his   sed head: Charles I of England, beheaded in 1649 by order of Parliamen

Shx.: Shakes

as to interprete   re/ Wellington: Pound corrects a misreading—in this case by his German eι ιor and translator Eva Hesse—of line 64, *Canto* LXXIX.

kummrad kumminkz': e. e. cummings (1894–1962), the American poet; longtime friend of Pound. "Kummrad," ironically, in allusion to cummings' *Eimi,* his record of months spent in Russia.

a mewZicial bloke: R. Murray Schafer?, Canadian composer and musicologist; editor of *Ezra Pound and Music* (New York: New Directions, 1977).

Ambrose time: St. Ambrose (*fl.* A.D. 340–97), became Bishop of Milan. Lacking "enc. noozitem from woptaly," it is not clear whom and what Pound refers to by "Alex" (Alexander) and "Roman arena."

Ammianus: Marcellinus Ammianus (*c.* 325–*c.* 391), a late Roman historian.

Alex and brahmin: the Gandhara period of Indian culture was the product of the interchange between Hellenistic Greek and native Indian traditions. *Cf.* Ambrose's *De Moribus Brachmanorum.*

Apollonius Tyana: (b. 4 B.C.), Hermetic mage. Philostratus wrote his *Life* (trans. Loeb Classical Library). See *Paideuma,* vol. 4, no. 1 (3–36), for discussion of Apollonius and the Rock-Drill *Cantos.*

giudeo Xtn: Judeo-Christianity.

Flaubert's sottisier: Dictionnaire des Idées Réçues, appendix to *Bouvard et Pécuchet.*

studies in contemporary mentality: a series of satiric short pieces on literature, society and the arts by Pound, appearing serially in *The New Age,* 1917–18.

MacLuhan: Herbert Marshall McLuhan (1911–81), media analyst, literary critic, social theorist. Pound probably refers to McLuhan's *The Mechanical Bride* (New York: Vanguard, 1951).

Condé Nast: Condé Nast (1874–1942), American publisher of *Vogue, House and Garden, Glamour,* etc., and hence a term for magazine publishers in general.

A Daughter of Confucius: Daughter of Confucius, A Personal History, by Su-Ling Wong and Earl Herbert Cressy (New York, 1952).

Vincent: Pound refers to H. P. Vincent of the Illinois Institute of Technology.

20

crack on p. 9: reference is to Pound's translation of Confucius' *The Unwobbling Pivot* (Square Dollar Series), p. 9, sec. XI, I: "to seek mysteries in the obscure, poking into magic and committing eccentricities in order to be talked about later; this I do not."

neo Kelley and sheets: neo-Shelley and Keats.

with about two "heaves," as you make Kung say: ? relation to Pound's "bust thru from quotidien into 'divine or permanent world'" (*Letters,* ed. D. D. Paige, p. 210).

21

Jim Stevens: (altered in Theobald's answer to James Stephens); a temporary member of St. Elizabeths circle; contributed a poem, "Shantih," to *Edge* 5. (*See also* letters of August 3, September 7, and September 15.)

Stevens: part of the first sentence (from "Stevens" to "POEM")has been excised.

Maverick: see Glossary.

Kuan Tzu: see Glossary.

Frobenius: Leo Frobenius, German anthropologist (1873–1938); his *Erlebte Erdteile* (Frankfurt, 1929) figures importantly in Pound's thought, especially the notion of "*Sagetrieb*," i.e., that poetry is a primary means of expressing and interpreting past cultural traditions. See *also Guide to Kulchur.*

de Angulo: Jaime de Angulo (1887–1950), California anthropologist and writer: *The Chontal Language* [dialect of Tequixistlan] (Vienna, 1925); *Indian Tales,* written and illustrated by Jaime de Angulo (Melbourne, 1954); *et al.* In the "Appendix—Poems by 5 Friends," *Pavannes and Divagations* (New York: New Directions, 1958), Pound includes a poem and drawing by Jaime de Angulo. Pound referred to him as "the American Ovid," and helped to secure publication of *Indians in Overalls* in Fred Morgan's *Hudson Review* (1950).

Waddell: Lt.-Col. L. A. Waddell (1854–1938), Scots linguist and Egyptologist: author of works on Sumer as a civilizing influence: *The Indo-Sumerian Seals Deciphered* (London: Luzac and Co., 1925); *The Aryan Origin of the Alphabet* (London: Luzac and Co., 1927); and *Egyptian Civilization, Its Sumerian Origin and Real Chronology* (London: Luzac and Co., 1930). See *Cantos* XCIV and XCVII.

Rock: see Glossary.

Goullart: see Glossary.

Patocki: Count Patocki, Polish Ambassador to the U.S.

EU-*which what:* meaning unclear. Eu (Greek): well, good, advantageous; Pound sometimes uses *which what* to mean "thing," "matter," etc.; perhaps "a good thing," "valuable items." (*cf. Paideuma* 9, no. 2, p. 356: "Have you ever tried to pack 13 years accumulations of which whats   benedictions: Ez P.")

Gruesen: John Joseph Gruesen; thesis: "The Philosophical Implications of Carl Gustav Jung's Individuation Process" (Washington, D.C.: Georgetown Univ., 1956).

lezOPE . . . : let's hope. At this time, Pound lumps together Jung and Freud as representatives of psychology. Yet *cf.* approving citation from Jung in "Foreword" to Pound's *Selected Cantos* (Faber and Faber, 1967), p. 9.

Father D'Arcy: Martin D'Arcy, S. J., author of *The Mind and Heart of Love* (London, 1945); *The Mystery of Love and Knowledge: Perennial Wisdom* (New York, 1959), *et al.*

N. Car.: North Carolina University Press.

The Point: see note to letter of May 28, 1957.

Pisani: Monsignor Pisani, archbishop in Rome. See Mary de Rachewiltz, *Discretions* (Atlantic-Little, Brown, 1971), pp. 13–14; and also *Canto* XCIII, ll. 8–21.

Canters: Cantos.

non raggiamo di lor: "let us not speak of them"; Dante, *Inferno* (Canto III); said of the "Trimmers," who fluctuate between parties and issues in order to appear to favor both sides.

one of 'em: one of the figures in Pound's Hell Cantos was Winston Churchill. Considering Pound's unabated loathing for Churchill, the reference could well be to him.

a certain power: Pound refers to England.

22

The Four Books: the four classic volumes of Confucianism: Confucius' *Unwobbling Pivot, The Great Digest, The Analects,* and Mencius's *On The Mind.*
N. H. P.'s comment: comment lost. Norman Holmes Pearson, 1914–75; professor of English, Yale University, and long-standing friend of H. D.; with Michael King, ed. *End to Torment, A Memoir of Ezra Pound* by H. D. (New York: New Directions, 1979); with W. H. Auden, *Poets of The English Language* (New York, 1950). Mentioned in *Canto* XCVI, l. 341. (See also letter of July 22, 1957.)

23

the enclosed from Macleish: enclosure lost.
NHP: Norman Holmes Pearson.
Ralph J'son: Ralph Johnson, a colleague of Theobald's at San Diego State University.
Schop.: Schopenhauer
the Pisan gesture: see letter of July 10, 1957.
Anthony West . . . on Japan: "Letter From Tokyo," *The New Yorker* (June 22, 1957), pp. 33–73.

24

intelligent note on Agassiz: "Intelligence Working in Nature" on Agassiz and the Square Dollar Series (attributed to Norman Holmes Pearson) appeared in *Edge* 3; however, see Gallup B54a.
West had done a Rebecca: wrote a travel piece in the fashion of Rebecca West?
H. G.: H. G. Wells.
canto: see *Canto* XLII, 3–5. Reference is to the statue of Queen Victoria at Buckingham Palace.
Kenner: Hugh Kenner.
deepchested of fatherland: see note to letter of June 11, 1957.
Eva: Eva Hesse, German translator of Pound, Eliot, cummings. Has written important studies of Pound's work, including *Ezra Pound, Von Sinn und Wahnsinn* (Munich: Kindler, 1978). Currently senior editor of *Paideuma.*
bag of Dukes: see letter of July 2, 1957 and *Canto* LXXIV, l. 398.
Rotocalcos: "trodden by wheel," printed sheets; *i.e.,* journals, or picture magazines in general?
Condé Nast: American magazine publisher; term used by Pound for all such.
Edg/: *Edge*; see Glossary.
Woodward's General Grant: William E. Woodward (1874–1950), American historian: *Meet General Grant* (New York, 1928); *A New American History* (New York, 1936); *Tom Paine: America's Godfather, 1737–1809* (New York, 1965); *et al.* See Pound's paragraphs on him in *Impact* (Chicago, 1960), pp. 256–59.

Brooks Adams . . . reading: Pound no doubt refers to Adams' *Law of Civilization and Decay* (? available "somewhere" at $1.25), which has been included in *Edge*'s "supplementary list" ("collateral, not necessarily curricular, reading"). *See* Glossary.

vile Reese/: Holroyd Reese, founder of Albatross Books (Hamburg-Paris-Bologna); bought Tauchnitz Editions.

Traxiniai: Pound translated Sophocles' *Women of Trachis* in 1953 (London, 1956; New York: New Directions, 1957).

Ichiro: Ichiro Kono, Japanese poet, friend of Theobald. Together they translated modern Japanese poetry.

Minoru: Umewaka Minoru, surviving master dancer of the Shogun's Noh troupe (after the Meiji Restoration of 1868); teacher of Ernest Fenollosa, 1878; preserved texts of many Noh plays with acting instructions, as well as masks, costumes, etc.; d. 1944? (*See Guide to Kulchur*, 217).

Following the tradition of continuing a master dancer's or actor's name, Kita Minoru performed with his troupe in Tokyo a proper Noh version of W. B. Yeats' *At the Hawk's Well* (1949, 1950 and 1952).

miss Lust: unidentified.

Ron Duncan: Ronald Duncan (1914–82), British poet; editor of *The Townsman* (London); his "Judas" appeared in *Edge 7*.

a perfectly SANE *trinity: see* note to letter of June 11, 1957.

koine ennoia/: "common sense" (*Greek*).

eggskeqsz: excuse.

nob. or *clerg.:* nobility or clergy.

Goullart HAD *a yank pubr/:* Peter Goullart, author of *Forgotten Kingdom*, did publish one book in U.S.A., *Land of the Lamas, Adventures in Secret Tibet* (New York: Dutton, 1959).

"Nweeee nwant": Pound's transcription of New England twang: "we want." Pound is stressing the fact that Americans are being ordered about by bureaucrats—a far cry from the civil liberties envisioned by Jefferson and Adams.

"il problema delle Tasse": "The tax problem." Originally printed in *Meridiano di Roma*, August 31, 1941 (one of Pound's 38 articles written mainly for that paper). Reprinted as *Orientamenti* (Venezia, 1944); entire issue destroyed by the publisher owing to the political and economic nature of the contents.

—ianiania: code word for works of popular scholarship in history, biography, etc.; ? deriving from "Lincolniania" (in Pound's letter of June 11, 1957 in reference to Carl Sandburg's *Lincoln*).

Van Dyne: ? Frederick Van Dyne (1861–1915), author of *A Treatise on the Law of Naturalization of the U.S.* (Washington, 1907).

25

Murray . . . to print the forgotten book: Forgotten Kingdom (London: John Murray, 1955) by Peter Goullart. See note to Pound's letter of June 10, 1957.

Jas Laughlin: James Laughlin, founder, president and publisher of New Directions Publishing Corporation. Close friend of Pound since the mid-1930s; the main publisher of Pound's works in all forms.

Kono: Ichiro Kono, Japanese poet and friend of Theobald.

26

without Muan pbo: Indian rite of self-rectification; cf. Cantos XCVIII (179), CIV (42–3), CXII (11–12).

Coomara swami: Amanda Kentich Coomaraswamy (1877–1947); author of a multitude of books on Indian art, Buddhism, Hinduism, etc.

T. H. Lawrence: probably D. H. Lawrence. (cf. Pound to Margaret Anderson, September 1917: ". . . F—— and Lawrence are stupid and blockheaded. Lawrence had less showing above the waterline when Hueffer took him up than Rodker has now. . . ." Letters, ed. D. D. Page, p. 122).

unscrewing the inscrutable: see Canto XCVIII, ll. 111–12.

"Dear Mark": Mark Hanna.

Carson Chang's book on neo-kung: Carson Chang, The Development of Neo-Confucian Thought (New York: Bookman Associates, 1957), 2 vols.

Dag H/: Dag Hammarskjöld, Secretary General of the United Nations in 1950's; see quote on Pound in Hammarskjöld's speech at the Museum of Modern Art, October 19, 1954, as quoted in This Difficult Individual, Ezra Pound by Eustace Mullins (New York, 1961), p. 340.

OOOzenstein the damned: F. D. Roosevelt.

kewpie doll: Dwight D. Eisenhower.

Junzaboro: see Glossary.

Odlin: Reno Odlin, artist influenced by Wyndham Lewis and member of St. Elizabeths circle; frequent contributor to Paideuma and Sagetrieb.

E. Miner: Earl Roy Miner, professor of English and Comparative Literature, Princeton; author of The Japanese Tradition in English and American Poetry (Princeton, 1958), et al.

"with one line marked": Theobald had enclosed with his August 24th letter to Pound a copy of a letter he had written to a friend covering various religious questions. Pound had bracketed, and pronounced "O.K." in the margin, the following sentence: ". . . it's a mistake to suppose it is necessary to leave the many behind when you clasp the One."

H. G.: H. G. Wells. Cf. Theobald's account of Wells with Pope's "Epistle to Dr. Arbuthnot," l. 182.

27

as Hogg says about Percy B: Thomas Jefferson Hogg, *Life of Percy Bysshe Shelley*,
   2 vols. (London, 1857). Vol. I, pp. 57–8, describes Shelley's report of a lecture
   on stones: "It was wonderfully tiring."

28

St. Bernard: cf. Dante's *Paradiso*, xxxii: "Let us [Bernard and Dante] turn our eyes
   to the Primal love . . . But . . . follow me with such affection that from my
   words thy heart be severed not," etc.
Anschauungs: "outlooks" (*German*).
Hawley: identity unknown.
JFC Fuller: U.S. Major General (b. 1878); author of *Armaments and History* (1945);
   The Second World War (1949); *et al.*
all econ/: all economics (books).
Unc Herbert: identity unclear.
Ari: Aristotle.

30

nipots of Unc. H: i.e., relations and descendents of "Uncle Herbert" (of letter of
   August 26, 1957).
"A Scholarly and Critical Journal": sub-title of *Twentieth Century Literature*, a
   copy of which Theobald had sent to Pound. (See Theobald's letter of August 26,
   1957).
Kulturausführung: "cultural presentation" (*German*).
Dilling: Mrs. Elizabeth Dilling (1894–?); author of *The Red Network* (1935); *The
   Roosevelt Red Record and Its Background* (1936); etc.
a gleam: reference is to a page in poetry textbook, *Reader and Writer* (1957?), ed.
   H. P. Vincent and H. Hayford. (Now out of print and unavailable to the editors.)
mélange adultère de tout: "adulterous [indiscriminate] mixing of everything
   together."
Mayo: Robert D. Mayo, professor (emeritus), Department of English, Northwestern
   University; taught regular courses on Pound and edited a Pound newsletter.

31

Henrietta Maria: Henrietta (Maria) Gostrey, a prominent figure in Henry James'
   The Ambassadors; here used metonymically for James' fiction as a whole.
Zielinsk Sib: La Sibylle by Thaddeus Zielinski; see Glossary.
Agresti: Olivia Agresti; see Glossary.
"Rome giv law . . .": cf. Zielinski, "'Avant l'avènement du Christ,' dit Clément
   d'Alexandrie, 'Dieu donna aux Hébreux la loi et aux Grecs la philosophie'" (p.
   7), which proposition Zielinski proceeds to demolish.
Plarr: Victor Gustav Plarr (1863–1929), member of The Rhymers' Club and author
   of *In the Dorian Mood* (1896); "Verog" in Pound's "Hugh Selwyn Mauberley."

Je-tzu: Jesù (Jesus).
H. J.: Henry James.
William instead of Henry: James.
Shapiro: Karl Shapiro, poet; editor, *The Prairie Schooner*, and of *Poetry* (March 1950–September 1955); took an active stand against the awarding of the Bollingen Prize to Pound.
Dilling: see note to previous letter of September 3rd.

33

a tex book: see note to letter of September 3rd.
Scudder on Agassiz: Samuel Hubbard Scudder (1837–1911), American naturalist, paleontologist, geologist; *Nomenclator Zoologicus* (1882); studied under Agassiz, 1857–62; Agassiz's assistant till 1864. Exact comment by Scudder on Agassiz uncertain.
Hayakawa: S. I. Hayakawa (1906–   ), popular writer on semantics (*Language in Action*, 1941); editor of *ETC*.
Dave: David Horton, co-publisher with John Kasper of "Square Dollar" Series; friend of Pound during the St. Elizabeths years.
Old Jerome: In 1874 Lord Randolph Churchill married Jennie, daughter of Leonard Jerome of New York. They had two sons, the eldest being Winston Churchill (b. 1874). For Jenny, *see Jennie: The Life and Times of Lady Randolph Churchill* by R. J. Martin, 2 vols. (New York, 1971): a *"femme de lettres,"* who wrote "teacup and saucer dramas" (*e.g., His Borrowed Plumes*, 1909).
Mihaelovitch: Draza Mihajlović, Colonel in Royal Yugoslav Army; with Tito, organized and led guerrilla resistance to the German invasion. After the war, the new Assembly found Mihajlović guilty of treason and had him executed on July 17, 1946.
connect ALL psychiatry with Beria program: L. P. Beria (1889–1953), head of Soviet Internal Security (OGPU). Pound's implication appears to be that psychiatry, like OGPU, represents an invasion of private life (*i.e.,* forms of thought-control), though he may mean to imply a direct connection between American psychiatry and Soviet secret police.
Edge 1 included the articles on the topic:
   "Attack Through the Mind," "Sub-threshold" and "Psychopolitics" (linked with Beria program) and *Edge* 3 included Jan A. van der Madé's "'Mental Illness' New Name for Nonconformity."
Rosanov: ? Dr. Aaron Joshua Rosanoff (*c.* 1911–12), writer on psychiatry, mental hygiene and insanity; or ? Mikhail Grigorevich Rozanov (1888–1938), Russian writer on Bolshevism; or ? Vasilii Vasilevich Rozanov (1856–1919), Russian writer on the Russian Revolution, Hebrew poetry and the Eastern Orthodox Church.
RIGHT older than man: Pound is suggesting that his right to choose his companions has been taken away by keeping him imprisoned; *cf.* W. B. Yeats, "The People,"

Collected Poems (New York, 1979), p. 149.

H. J.: Henry James. "H. Sr" is the novelist's father, Henry, who was much interested in the thought of Emanuel Swedenborg, and wrote a book about him: *The
Secret of Swedenborg* (Boston, 1869).

Chavez, Tutt, V. Vanti: linguistic variants of Javits?

34

Mariannah: Marianne Moore.

O. R. A.: Olivia Rossetti Agresti; *see* Glossary.

Haywire: H. Hayford.

M. S.: Marcella Spann.

HER text book: *Confucius to Cummings: An Anthology of Poetry.*

Mond: possibly Sir Robert Ludwig Mond (1868–1938), British chemist and in-
dustrialist; head of largest British Chemical Trust; executive in nickel industry.
Pound believed that the Monds, Jewish financiers to his eyes, had forced Ford
Madox Ford out of the editorship of the *English Review* (*see Canto* CIV); also
see Cantos LXXVIII, which quotes, presumably, Robert Mond, and LXXXIV,
which connects "Imperial Chemicals" with munitions-makers.

Tseng has just resigned from Tunghai: see note to letter of June 11, 1957.

Cauvinite: Calvinist?; Cohenite? (both the same to Pound?).

Fred Manning: Frederic Manning, Australian poet and writer. Pound mentions his
Scenes and Portraits commendingly; *see Pound/Joyce* (New York: New Directions, 1970), p. 65, and note 8.

Yittischer Charleston Band: A music-hall type song, composed by Pound and
T. S. Eliot in the early 1920's. Printed in Louis Zukofsky's *An "Objectivists"
Anthology* (1932) as "Yittischer Charleston." *See* letter of Pound to Zukofsky
(ed. Barry Ahearn) of November 24–5, 1930, appearing in *Montemora* 8, pp.
173–4; *see also* Gallup B29.

wrong line: Pound continues from the line above ending with "toyu."

F. M.: Ford Madox Ford.

止 : "to come at ultimate truth" (Chinese).

Agresti: see Glossary.

anagogic velleities: spiritual apathy.

damnᴌieing again: Time Magazine (September 9, 1957, p. 48) reported Pound as
saying that "Papa Hemingway knows how to write, but he's dishonest."
Hemingway responded in a letter to Dorothy Pound: "I could read each day that
he denounced me and would no more believe it than I would believe that we
did not live in Rue Notre Dame des Champs in the old days" (*The Caged
Panther*, p. 53).

Lice's paper: Henry Luce's magazines *Time* or *Life*?

the turk's article: by the "professingly benevolent" Gun in *Il Tempo*, August 29,
1957. (*See* letter of October 17, 1957).

kepp'n me kepp'n: Walt Whitman's "O Captain! My Captain!"

35

that congressman: Usher L. Burdick of North Dakota, who introduced "House Resolution 403," calling for full investigation of Pound case, August 21, 1957.

B. L. Mayo: Pound was referring to Robert Mayo, who edited a Pound newsletter.

Kono: Ichiro Kono.

36

tripartito: Axis.

Ito: Michio Ito (1892–1961); traditional Japanese dancer, discovered in late 1915 by Gordon Craig, Yeats and Pound; performed in Yeats' *At the Hawk's Well*, April 4, 1916. See Helen Caldwell, *Michio Ito: The Dancer and His Dances* (University of California Press, 1977).

non son tutti usignoli: "they are not all nightingales" (*Italian*).

Chennevière: Paul Chennevière. "The young party of intelligence in Paris, a party now just verging on the threshold of middle age, is the group that centered about 'L'Effort Libre.' It contains Jules Romains, Vildrac, Duhamel, Chennevière, Jouvre, and their friends."—Pound's review of Jouvre in *Poetry* (February 1912). See also *Canto* LXXX, l. 458, and *Pavannes*, pp. 133–4.

Flint: F(rank) S(tewart) Flint (1885–1960), Imagist poet, critic, member of Pound's London circle in the early years (1910–14).

e. e. c.: e. e. cummings.

La Canaille Lιττтeraire: "the literary riff-raff" (*French*).

Junior Anth/: Confucius to Cummings: An Anthology of Poetry, ed. by Ezra Pound and Marcella Spann (New York: New Directions, 1958), 340 pp., including appendices.

Chapman: George Chapman (1559?–1634), English poet and dramatist, translator of Homer's *Iliad* (1598–1611) and *Odyssey* (1616).

Vince: Professor Vincent Miller, one of Marcella Spann's teachers. His "Syllabus for students" is included in Appendix ii of *Confucius to Cummings*.

Rouse: W. H. D. Rouse (1863–1950), British educator, writer, translator of Greek literature: *The Story of Odysseus* (1937); *The Story of Achilles* (1938). See Pound's letters to Rouse on translating Homer in D. D. Paige's *The Letters of Ezra Pound*.

Ogilby: John Ogilby, Scottish translator of Virgil (1668); also *The Iliad* (1660); *The Odyssey* (1665).

Golding: Arthur Golding (1536–1605), English translator of Ovid's *Metamorphoses* (often noted by Pound as "the most beautiful book in the language").

Gavin D/: Gavin Douglas (1474?–1552), Scottish poet; his translation of Virgil's *Aeneid* (1553) Pound considered "magnificent," full of "richness and fervor" (*Confucius to Cummings*, p. 34).

Merchant: W. Moelwyn Merchant; see note on "Welchman eating on Folger," letter of September 24, 1957; see also Gallup C1909.

Folger: Folger Library of Shakespeare material in Washington, D.C.

traductions: "translations" (French).

Bion, F. Fawkes: Francis Fawkes (1720–77), English poet and divine; his translation of minor Greek poets, including Bion, appeared in 1761.

Theoc.: Theocritus (*fl.* 3rd cent. B.C.), Greek pastoral poet. In *Confucius to Cummings* the 1684 edition of Theocritus translated by Thomas Creech (published by Stephens) is included in excerpt.

Sixe Idyllia. Barnes Oxford 1588: Sixe idillia, printed at Oxford by Joseph Barnes, 1588.

Herrick: Robert Herrick (1591–1674), English lyric and erotic poet.

Waller: Edmund Waller (1606–87), English lyric poet.

Rose: allusion to Waller's "Go lovely rose," included in *Confucius to Cummings.*

Lawes: Henry Lawes (1595–1662), English composer; supplied the incidental music for Comus in 1634. (*See also Canto* LXXXI, "libretto" section.) Reference here is to Waller's "To Mr. Henry Lawes," included in *Confucius to Cummings.*

Maverick: Lewis Adams Maverick, sinologist; *see* Glossary.

Williamson: Henry Raymond Williamson, *Wang An Shih* [1021–86], *A Chinese Statesman and Educationalist of the Sung Dynasty* (London, 1935–7).

Plologue: Chaucer's "Prologue" to *Canterbury Tales.*

Hero: Marlowe's *Hero and Leander* (*c.* 1590).

Fordie: F. M. Ford.

Mavrogordato: John Mavrogordato (1882–?), Greek poet and translator; *Elegies and Songs* (1934); translator of *Poems of Konstantinos Kabaphea (Cavafy),* with notes (New York: New Directions, 1952).

Shx/: Shakespeare's.

"Little Yamm . . .": parody of W. Blake's *Songs of Innocence.*

Xtism: Christianity.

casus belli: cause of war.

Kung's Florilegium: Confucius' *Book of Odes.*

Giot/ and Bot: Giotto and Botticelli.

Barbara Frietchie: ballad by John Greenleaf Whittier; included in *Confucius to Cummings.*

Bayard Taylor's Faust: Bayard Taylor (1825–78), American poet, translated Goethe's *Faust* into English, 2 vols. (Boston, 1870–1) in the original meters; considered for years the standard translation.

seal: Pound's orange colored seal, with which he signed some of his letters, is acrophonic. It consists of three components, having values as follows:

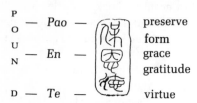

P			
O	— Pao —		preserve
			form
U			grace
N	— En —		gratitude
D	— Te —		virtue

37

man in the iron mask: Time Magazine (September 9, 1957) printed what it claimed
was an interview of Pound by *Il Tempo* (Italian newspaper). See note on "NOBLE
BLAST," letter of October 4, 1957.

Yvor Winters: American critic and poet.

your son: Omar S. Pound, poet, translator of Persian poetry.

Bulganin: Nikolai Bulganin (1895–1975); after Stalin's death, vice-premier in
Malenkov's government; premier after the latter's resignation, 1955; ousted by
Khrushchev, 1958.

enclosed from the nice-sounding Maverick: enclosure lost.

38

mahabharattz: from *Mahabharata;* Pound here means something like: "you literati with Indian leanings."

Ghose: Kali Mohan Ghose; pupil of Tagore's; translated "Certain Poems of Kabir"
with Pound; published in *Modern Review* (Calcutta), June, 1913.

Kalidasa: Hindu dramatist and lyric poet, 5th century A.D.

to particulars: cf. Pound in *The Exile,* no. 2 (Autumn 1927): ". . . the lack in
America of any habit of connecting or correlating *any* act or *thought* to *any*
main principle whatsoever; the ineffable rudderlessness of that people." (*Impact,* ed. N. Stock [Chicago, 1960], p. 221.)

Benton: see Glossary.

Niebuhr: Reinhold Niebuhr (1892–1971), American theologian; *see* earlier letter
of Pound of June 17, 1957.

Lubin: see Glossary entry for Agresti.

Luce, Lice or Spewlitzer: Henry Luce, publisher of *Time, Life, Fortune* magazines.
"Spewlitzer," i.e., Pulitzer: Joseph Pulitzer (1847–1911) established the annual
Pulitzer Prize for literature (and drama, music, journalism).

perfidious Gun in "Tempo": interviewer of Pound for *Il Tempo.* (See also
Theobald's letter, September 18, 1957.)

Giovannini: Giovanni Giovannini; Pound is referring here to Giovannini's peppery "The Strange Case of Ezra Pound," *New Times* (Melbourne), August 26,
1955, pp. 194–6, see Glossary.

Comfort: Howard Comfort (1904–?), taught Latin at Haverford College; author of
Studies in Byzantine Land-Leases (Haverford, 1939).

Chatel: John Chatel, visitor of Pound's at St. Elizabeths; contributed "Bouvard:
Flaubert on Money" to *Edge* 7.

Mat/A: Matthew Arnold.

Bret Harte: Francis Brett Hart (1836–1902), American writer of humorous Western
fiction and poems.

Sill: Edward Rowland Sill (1841–87), American minor poet and critic: *The Her-
mitage and Other Poems* (1868); *The Venus of Milo and Other Poems* (1883); *et
al.*

a welchman eating on Folger: William Moelwyn Merchant, Fulbright Fellow, 1957; Fellow Folger Library, 1957; Professor of English Language and Literature, University of Exeter, Devon; author of *Shakespeare and The Artist* (Oxford University Press, 1959), *et al.*

eating on Folger: i.e., supported by a Folger Library fellowship.

Coke: see Glossary.

last two engleshmen: i.e., two other Fulbright scholars; identities unknown.

still vote fer Mark Hanna: Marcus Alonso Hanna (1837–1914); leader of Conservative wing of the Republican Party in that period.

meta ta phusikaaaa: "*meta ta physica,*" metaphysics; i.e., Greek, as opposed to Jewish, thought ("Mesopotamia") [Greek].

D. P.: Dorothy Pound.

H. J.: Henry James.

COM . . . . . . *patrioт: cf.* opening anecdote in Hugh Kenner's *The Pound Era,* pp. 3–4.

old BITCH: statue of Queen Victoria at Buckingham Palace.

Sagetrieb: Pound defines *Sagetrieb* as "the oral tradition" in *Canto LXXXIX.*

Bennett: Arnold Bennett (1867–1931), British novelist.

39

Basho: Bashō (1643–94), Japanese poet, "founder" of the modern school of *haiku.*

Taikan: Takuan? (late 16th century—*fl.* 1644), Zen master in calligraphy and swordsmanship.

40

befo-brek: before breakfast.

three buzzards: i.e., three associate editors (or compilers) who "divided . . ." etc.

Skeat: Walter William Skeat (1835–1912), English philologist and specialist in Anglo-Saxon.

virtuous profl: i.e., J. Theobald, evidently mentioned anonymously in *Edge* by Pound.

Vince: Vincent Miller, a former teacher of Marcella Spann, helped edit, and contributed an appendix to, *Confucius to Cummings.*

tu ne quaesaris: "you don't ask" (with sense of "pray" or "beseech") [Latin].

two frogs: see Michael Reck, *Ezra Pound: A Close-Up,* p. 166.

41

Bunting: Basil Bunting, English poet; author of *Poems 1950, The Spoils, First Book of Odes, Briggflatts, Collected Poems* (1968), *et al.* Pound's *Guide to Kulchur* is dedicated to him and Louis Zukofsky, "strugglers in the desert."

42

NOBLE BLAST: Pound refers to a letter written by Theobald to *Time Magazine* protesting various assertions in their report (September 9, 1957) of an interview of Pound by *Il Tempo.* "I'm like the Man in the Iron Mask," Pound is reported as saying. "My Mask imprisons my thoughts and smothers my voice." And on writers: "Papa Hemingway knows how to write, but he's dishonest." Theobald's letter was never printed by *Time,* but did appear in Louis Dudek's *Delta,* no. 2 (January, 1958):

Sir:

It has come to my attention that your representative intruded on Ezra Pound without his sanction. That might have been pardonable (though not every journalist who strolls into St. Elizabeths Hospital is at liberty to take Mr. Pound's time) if the resulting interview had been reported with any adherence to the truth. It was not.—There are some of us who do not share at all Mr. Pound's views, to put it mildly, but who also do not enjoy seeing him taken advantage of. Knowing that it was impossible to do the prisoner's person more damage than has been done, was it Time's object to commit the sole remaining injury—poison his relations with his friends? It is of little consequence that Mr. Pound never said that Hemingway was dishonest, and that he never applied to himself such a ludicrously un-Poundian piece of self-pity as the "man in the iron mask" idiocy. Time will not feel it necessary to retract, or even to print this letter, written merely to convey the assurance that such distortions at the expense of a person of Mr. Pound's eminence invariably backfire.

John Theobald

H. *Louce:* Henry R. Luce (1898–1967), publisher of *Life, Time, Fortune.*

Barney: Bernard Baruch (1870–1965), American financier and speculator; had a strong political influence on F. D. Roosevelt and Winston Churchill; called "advisor of presidents." Pound had unbounded contempt for him.

I don't see why all construction: Pound is saying that his twenty years' work fashioning a new prosody was hardly a variation on an English pentameter base, but "construction" of new rhythmic measures.

Landor's speculation: unclear reference to Walter Savage Landor's "speculation" on lost works by Ovid, written in exile, in a foreign tongue.

Shx Jacques: Shakespeare. (*Cf. ABC of Reading,* p. 187: "Jacques Père, spelling it Shaxpear, because J is either pronounced hard or confused with I. . . ."); and *Canto* CII, ll. 39–40: "'Jacques Pere' on a sign near Le Portel,/ and belgians would pronounce it."

there WAS a wop: Italian scholar; identity unknown.

nex issue: Esquire (December, 1957), "The Sound and Fury," pp. 53–4. See especially letter by G. Giovannini.

jaκκαmmerz: jackhammers.

nome. cog/ed indirizzi: i.e., "name, surname and addresses."
Dudek broadcast: C.B.C. broadcast: "The Letters of Ezra Pound" (Wednesday, September 14, 1957). A general review and appreciation of Pound's literary career, by Louis Dudek, Department of English, McGill University. Pound was very pleased with the summary, calling it "magnificent," "possibly the best yet." Reprinted in: D/K Some Letters of Ezra Pound, Louis Dudek (Montreal, 1974).

43

betrayal of the U.S. in 1913: see P.S. to letter of June 3, 1957.
Hem's timing: see previous commentary on this section.
Page: Giorgio Nelson Page, Pound's supervisor on Rome Radio.
Perkins: Frances Perkins (1882–1965), American public official; member of the Roosevelt Cabinet, 1933; Secretary of Labor under F. D. R.; influenced New Deal economic programs. "For 25 years Steed [H. W., British editor, BBC broadcaster during W.W. II] has resisted abundance economy . . . and now he hears it from Perkins, that AFTER the War, after the Jews get control again . . . the old bleeders will all be Christ child, and Santy Claus." (Ezra Pound Speaking)
Hopkins: Harry Hopkins (1890–1946), Secretary of Commerce, 1938–40; close friend of F. D. R.; carried out "missions" to Russia and Britain during World War II.
correspondent in western bughouse: identity unknown.
prince-indices: price-indices?
Whorf: Benjamin Lee Whorf (1897–1941), American linguist; author of Language, Thought and Reality (Cambridge, 1956).
Ryozo: Ryozo Iwasaki, Japanese translator and editor of Pound's Selected Poems (Tokyo, 1945).
Sheri M.: Sheri Martinelli, Greenwich Village painter and Poundian disciple during St. Elizabeths years; Pound dubbed her "La Martinelli." (A portrait of Pound by Sheri Martinelli serves as frontispiece of the present volume.) Pound arranged publication of a small book of her paintings, La Martinelli (Milan, 1955).
éplucher: "to examine minutely" (French).
A Jap English studies/: The Rising Generation (Tokyo), a literary journal edited by Bunsho Jugaku and published by Kenkyusha Publishing Co. (one of the major publishers in Japan). Pound refers to vol. CIII, no. 10 (October 1, 1957) which contained a "Special Section" on William Blake.

44

Keynes: John Maynard Keynes (1883–1946); British economist, with Bloomsbury affiliations; author of Treatise on Money (1930); General Theory of Employment, Interest and Money (1936); strongly influenced New Deal economics.
Parrington: Vernon Louis Parrington (1891–1929), Professor of English, Univer-

sity of Michigan and Columbia University; author of *Main Currents in American Thought*, 2 vols., 1927.

Julian Huxley: Julian Huxley (1887–1975), British biologist; *Essays of a Biologist* (1923); *Evolutionary Ethics* (1943); etc. First director-general of UNESCO (1946–8).

Irving Babbitt: Irving Babbitt (1865–1933), American professor of French, Harvard University; leader of "New Humanism" movement in the twenties; author of *Rousseau and Romanticism* (1919); teacher of T. S. Eliot, 1909–10.

Hayakawa: see note to letter of September 8, 1957.

Sapir: Edward Sapir (1884–1930), American anthropologist and linguist, University of Chicago and Yale University; made linguistic studies of several Indian tribes of N.W. United States; author, *Language, an Introduction to the Study of Speech* (New York, 1921); etc.

Fabre d'Olivet: Antoine Fabre d'Olivet (1767–1825), French philologist: *The Hebraic Tongue Restored* (1815–16); translated Byron's *Cain* (1823).

Housman: A(lfred) E(dward) Housman (1859–1936), the British poet (*A Shropshire Lad*, 1896). "The Name and Nature of Poetry" was a lecture delivered at Cambridge in 1933. Theobald refers to Pound's "Mr. Housman at Little Bethel" (*Literary Essays*, pp. 66–73).

Other Voices, Other Rooms: Semi-autobiographical novel by Truman Capote, 1948; author also of *Breakfast at Tiffany's* (1958); etc.

45

C. H. D.: C. H. Douglas; see Glossary.

Sinc. Lewis' character: the central character in Sinclair Lewis's novel *Babbitt* (New York, 1922).

wot Jef/wrut to Crawford in 1816: Pound quotes from this letter in *Kulchur*: ". . . and if the national bills issued, be bottomed (as is indispensable) on pledges of specific taxes for their redemption within certain and moderate epochs, and be of '*proper denomination*' for '*circulation*,' no interest on them would be necessary or just, because they would answer to every one of the purposes of the metallic money withdrawn and replaced by them."—Thomas Jefferson (1816, letter to Crawford). *See Guide to Kulchur* (New York: New Directions, 1970), p. 354.

Eisenschemmel: Otto Eisenschemmel (1880–1903), author of *Why Was Lincoln Murdered?* (Boston, 1937). A serious, if journalistic, enquiry into the circumstances and events surrounding the death of Lincoln.

TRY *it*: i.e., the Whorf ms, "A linguistic consideration of thinking in primitive communities."

Oxford Odyssey: John Theobald's meditative long poem, *An Oxford Odyssey* (Janus, 1955), about an Oxford undergraduate, "stroke" on the sculling team, trying to get away from Oxford and reach the sea (i.e., the infinite).

Miles Payne: see Theobald's "Foreword" to the present correspondence.

che il giudeo fra voi di voi non ride: "that the Jew [who lives] among you doesn't laugh at you."

Meacham: Harry M. Meacham, president of the Poetry Society of Virginia, a poet and businessman who worked to interest many literati and politicians on Pound's behalf. He wrote to Dorothy Pound urging that Pound "should write MacLeish, Cummings, Dr. Williams or Eliot, pointing out (as he did to me) that he does not support Kasper" and that this "should be leaked to a friendly newspaper (if we can find one). . . . If he agrees I might be able to arrange for an interview along these lines" (*The Caged Panther*, p. 57). Pound's repudiation is characteristically resolute.

consuete disc.: consuèto discaro? (Italian); "an unpleasant habit," *i.e.,* "an old story"?

for the vol/: i.e., An Oxford Odyssey.

Scarfoglio: Carlo Scarfoglio, anti-fascist journalist who wrote (in *Mercure de France,* April, 1949) in defense of Pound's radio activities; *see* Gallup D81b.

Beaudoin: Kenneth Lawrence Beaudoin (1913–   ), Southern poet, author of *On Hot Summer Afternoons and Other Poems* (San Diego, 1956). (Mention of Yu Suwa not found.)

Yu Suwa: contemporary (b. 1929) Japanese poet; co-editor of Japanese literary magazine *WILL.*

Muggerzoon: Poundese for "magazine" (entitled *Kast?*).

HEKASTA: "particulars" (Greek).

Ryozo Iwasaki: see letter of October 17, 1957.

that tumpty tum question: see letters of October 1 and 4, 1957.

Beddoes: Thomas Lovell Beddoes, who worked to "break the pentameter" 100 years before Eliot? His metrical variety and freedom (*see Death's Jest Book*) make Eliot's line seem to "limp" by contrast? *cf. Canto* LXXX:

> Curious, is it not, that Mr. Eliot
> has not given more time to Mr. Beddoes
>   (T. L.) prince of morticians
> where none can speak his language . . .

cf. Beddoes:

> Thou are so silent, lady; and I utter
> Shadows of words, like to an ancient ghost,
> Arisen out of sea-wrapt centuries
> Where none can speak his language.

> *Death's Jest Book,* I, II (178–81)

46

Cole: G(eorge) D(ouglas) H(oward) Cole, British economist and novelist; author of *What Marx Really Meant* (1934); *Socialism in Evolution* (1938); *et al.*

Stella: Stella Bowen, artist, writer, common-law wife of Ford Madox Ford. Her *Drawn From Life* (1941) contains numerous prose portraits of contemporary personalities such as Max Beerbohm, Alfred Adler, Ezra Pound, *et al.*

Phyllis: Phyllis Bottome, novelist, essayist, friend of Pound from the London years, and later in Italy.

Coke and Blackstone: see Glossary.

G. B. S.: George Bernard Shaw.

G. Giov: Giovanni Giovannini; *see* Glossary.

Institutes: Pound here means the third part ("Concerning High Treason") for "2nd."

1878: see Canto LXXXVIII, l. 86, and ll. 113–15; and *cf.:* "After the assassination of Lincoln, President Johnson did not have the means to maintain fiscal liberty. In 1878, a Congressman expressed, or explained, his position by saying that he wanted to keep at least a part of the national debt in circulation as non-interest bearing currency." ("Economic Nature of the United States," in *Selected Prose, 1909–65,* ed. Cookson (1973), p. 179.) The Congressman referred to was Pound's grandfather Thaddeus Coleman Pound (*cf.* "A Visiting Card," *Selected Prose,* pp. 310, 325).

Miltosh: i.e., John Milton.

Eisenschemmel: see letter of October 24 ("or something"), 1957.

Benton: Thomas Hart Benton, U.S. senator; *see* Glossary.

Van Buren: Martin Van Buren, U.S. president; *see* Glossary.

Carl: Carl Lorraine.

"sorry for": i.e., for Pound's imprisonment in St. Elizabeths.

Leopold Loeb: famous murder trial of two young men; their lawyer was Clarence Darrow.

Maggie Charter: Magna Charta; *cf.* Coke in Glossary.

S. Carolina is emotional: Pound is possibly referring to reported disturbances over school in S. Carolina, where there was no integration, and where the trustees of one school district were under Federal Court order to begin it. (*See Time Magazine,* September 23, 1957.) John Kasper had given segregationist speeches there.

Ox Od/: Theobald's long meditative poem, *An Oxford Odyssey* (Janus, 1955), about an Oxford undergraduate.

Kung/ Pivot and Analects: reference is to Pound's translations of Confucius: *The Unwobbling Pivot* and *The Analects of Confucius.* Both were issued in the "Square Dollar" series.

47

"bag of Dukes": tobacco, "Duke's mixture" (according to Edwards and Vasse). *See Canto* LXXIV, l. 398.

Witch of Atlas: Shelley's mythological and fanciful poem (1820).

Wheelwright: Philip Wheelwright (1901–73), professor of philosophy and literature (U.C.R., 1954–70); *The Burning Fountain* (Indiana, 1962); edited a volume of the fragments of Heraclitus.

Olaf Stapledon: Olaf Stapledon (1886–1950), writer of science fiction: *Last and First Men* (New York, 1931); *Star Maker* (New York, 1937). Also wrote anthropological and scholarly studies: *A Modern Theory of Ethics* (New York, 1929); *Youth and Tomorrow* (London, 1946).

48

Major Kehoe: Major Donald E. Keyhoe, U.S. Marine Corps (ret.). From 1949, his main interest was in "Flying Saucers," concerning which he wrote two widely discussed books: *Flying Saucers from Outer Space* (1953) and *The Flying Saucer Conspiracy* (1955).

49

inside the soul: cf. *Canto* CXIII, l. 84.

ens: "being" *(Latin)*.

ne ultra crepidam: (crepitam?) "I shall rattle on no farther" *(Latin)*.

Gordon: David Gordon.

settimo cielo: "seventh heaven" *(Italian)*.

50

Tocqueville: Comte Alexis Henri de Tocqueville (1805–59); French statesman and author: *Democracy in America* (1835).

J. J.: James Joyce?, or Jean-Jacques Rousseau?

T. S. E.: T. S. Eliot.

R. A.: identity unclear. [Richard Aldington?]

"Sweeniad": parody by Myra Buttle *(pseud.* of Victor Purcell) published in 1957 by the Sycamore Press, N.Y. A rather flip and inept *mélange* of verses satirizing the work of such moderns as Eliot, Joyce, Pound, *et al.*

fais q'ou 'ouldra: "do what you want" (quote from Rabelais' *Gargantua*).

C. L.: Carolus Linnaeus. *Cf. Canto* CXIII: ". . . to walk with Mozart, Agassiz and Linnaeus/ 'neath overhanging air under sun-beat/ Here take thy mind's space. . . ."

Col. Ergot: identity unknown.

51

Rachewiltz translation: Boris de Rachewiltz, Pound's son-in-law, archeologist and ethnologist, did several translations of hieroglyphic texts, including *The Book of The Dead* (from the Turin manuscript). His Italian translation of a number of Egyptian hieroglyphs and inscriptions formed the basis of Pound and Noel Stock's *Love Poems of Ancient Egypt.*

Scheiwiller: Vanni Scheiwiller, Pound's Italian publisher (located in Milan); published 15 of Pound's books, as well as some by Boris and Mary de Rachewiltz, and their son (Walter Siegfried) and daughter (Patrizia).

Saitic: ancient Egyptian (XXVI dynasty).

Budge: E. A. J. Wallis Budge (1857–1934), Orientalist and curator of Egyptian and Assyrian antiquities at the British Museum (1894–1924); author of numerous books on Egyptology and translations of Egyptian texts.

These two young men: Boris de Rachewiltz and Vanni Scheiwiller.

Glossary

ADAMS, BROOKS: American historian (1848–1927), born Quincy, Mass.; direct descendent of John Adams and brother of Henry. Author of: *The Law of Civilization and Decay* (London, 1895; rev. ed. New York, 1897); *America's Economic Supremacy* (1900); *The New Empire* (1902); and *Theory of Social Revolutions* (1913); edited, and wrote an introduction to, Henry Adams' *The Degradation of the Democratic Dogma* (1919).

Pound championed *The Law of Civilization and Decay*, which emphasized the role played by money and usury in the rise and fall of civilizations. An anonymous review of the book in *Edge* 1 (p. 32) states: "His cyclic vision of the West shows us a consecutive struggle against four great rackets, namely the exploitation of the fear of the unknown (black magic, etc.), the exploitation of violence, the exploitation or monopolization of cultivable land, and the exploitation of money." See Pound's *A Visiting Card* (1942).

AGASSIZ, LOUIS: Swiss-American geologist and naturalist (1807–73); taught zoology at Harvard University. Stressed the need for science of direct observation of, and active contact with, the natural world. Author of: *Recherches sur les poissons fossiles* (1833–43); *Études sur les glaciers* (1840); and *Contributions to the Natural History of the United States* (1857–62).

"Intelligence Working in Nature" (*see* Gallup B54a) dealing with Agassiz appeared in *Edge* 3.

AGRESTI, OLIVIA ROSSETTI: daughter of William Michael Rossetti, brother of the pre-Raphaelite poet Dante Gabriel Rossetti. Translated into Italian Pound's essay "What Is Money For?" ("A che serve il danaro?" *Meridiano di Roma*, VI, 30 (July 27, 1941). [*See* Gallup D134.] Her "Pages of Memoir" appeared in *Edge* 4 and her "David Lubin" appeared in *Edge* 8. [*See* Mary de Rachewiltz, *Discretions* (Boston, 1971), pp. 165 *ff*.]

Olivia Agresti was an astute commentator on social and economic problems, especially those of modern Italy, and was the author of a study of the internationalist David Lubin (Boston, 1922). Pound wrote of her to Harry Meacham (September 24, 1957): "[She] was interpreter at Versailles, and at 83 knows as much of Europe as anyone. And of the fascist regime, which she did not wholly approve but which she does justice for constructivity" (*The Caged Panther* [N.Y., 1967], p. 50).

BENTON, THOMAS HART: (1782–1858), born Hillsboro, North Carolina; U.S. Senator (1821–51). Played influential role in the administrations of Andrew Jackson and Martin Van Buren. Proponent of "hard money," he was a prominent power in the successful war on the Bank of the United States. He also had the ratio of silver to gold revised (1834), thus bringing gold back into circulation. Drew up the Jacksonian "Specie Circular," legalized in an executive order (1836), requiring that public lands be paid for exclusively in hard currency. His currency measures intended to discourage land speculation and encourage the actual settlement and development of Western land. Supported legislation aiding settlers by reduction in the price of government land and suppression of land speculation; favored gradual abolition of slavery (1850). Author of *Thirty Years' View, 1820–1850*, 2 vols. (1854–6); compiled *An Abridgement of the Debates of Congress from 1789 to 1856*, 16 vols. (1857–61).

See especially Benton's "Speech Against the Renewal of the Charter of the Bank of the United States" (1831) and Chap. XXXI, vol. 2, of his autobiographical *Thirty Years' View* to account for the force of Pound's comments.

BLACKSTONE, SIR WILLIAM: English jurist and legal historian (1723–1780), author of *Commentaries on the Laws of England* (1765–9), a work that brought the formless bulk of English law into clarity and order, ranking with the achievements of his distinguished predecessors in the field: Sir Edward Coke and Sir Matthew Hale. Written in a clear style, this work set out to demonstrate that as a system of justice, English law was comparable to Roman law and continental civil law.

An advertisement (perhaps written by Pound) for a Blackstone pamphlet to appear in the Square Dollar Series (but which never did) praised him as part of "the great heritage aimed at government according to law, humanized by mechanism for preventing injustice by application of the decreed formulae in peculiar cases not fully foreseen by the legislators." Listed by Pound as one of the essential books "dealing with history and philosophy of law" (*Guide to Kulchur*, p. 352).

COKE, SIR EDWARD: English jurist (1552–1634); championed common law against encroachments of the royal prerogative; declared null and void royal proclamations that were contrary to law; leader of the popular faction in opposition to both James I and Charles I. Prominent in the drafting of the *Petition of Rights* (1628). Author of: *Reports* (a series of detailed commentaries on cases in common law) and the *Institutes of the Laws of England* (1628), the second part of which is based on the *Magna Charta* of 1225.

Pound appears to have discovered Coke toward the end of his St. Elizabeths stay, citing Coke on treason in *The European* (August 1958). Yet Coke's principle of "Misprision of Treason" is cited in Pound's Rome Radio broadcast of April 23, 1942. Pound constantly stressed the reading of Coke's *Institutes* and strongly recommended Catherine Drinker Bowen's life of Coke, *The Lion and The Throne*. In *Canto* CVII, Coke is referred to as "the clearest mind ever in England."

DOUGLAS, MAJOR CLIFFORD HUGH: (1829–1952), British economist and originator of the theory of Social Credit, which holds that maldistribution of wealth due to insufficient purchasing power is the reason for economic depressions and World Wars. Douglas hoped that his economic system could help escape the cycle of inflation and government debt, as well as avoid resorting to collectivist authoritarianism. He first expressed his ideas in writing in *The Organizer* (1917) and *The English Review* (1918). Assisted by A. R. Orage, he continued to publish articles serially in *The New Age*, gathered together in *Economic Democracy* and *Credit-Power and Democracy*.

Pound's economic thinking was strongly influenced by the views of Douglas and Orage, which he continued to develop. *See* Pound's "Obituary: A. R. Orage" and "In the Wounds," *Selected Prose*, pp. 437–51.

Edge: Australian literary magazine founded by Noel Stock in October 1956, to which Pound was a frequent anonymous contributor. There were eight issues published (nos. 1–8), the last one appearing in October 1957. A sampling of the articles appearing follows:

> *Edge* 1: "Five French Poems" by Ezra Pound; "Mencius" by David Gordon; "Richard of St. Victor" by S. V. Yankowski; "Poems of Tu Fu" by Chao Tze-chiang; "The High Bridge Above the Tagus River at Toledo" by W. C. Williams.
>
> *Edge* 2:"The Sibyl" by Thaddeus Zielinski.
>
> *Edge* 3: "Tang & Sung Poems" by D. R. Wang; "Catullus" by W. Fleming; "Credit" by McNair Wilson; "Ezra Pound Case" by Jan A. Van der Madé; "Suez Canal: Money" by Essad Essain.
>
> *Edge* 4: "Pages of Memoir" by Olivia Rossetti Agresti; "The Church & Usury" by Henry Swabey; "Laforgue & Jammes" by Charles Guenther; "In Captivity" by B. Mussolini.
>
> *Edge* 5: "Poem" by Nishiwaki Junzaburo; "Scotus Erigena" by Henry Swabey; "Opus 1, No. 1" by Ralph Reid; "Man of Yalta" by Georges Ollivier.
>
> *Edge* 6: "Leoun" by Jean Cocteau, trans. by Alan Neame.
>
> *Edge* 7: "Judas" by Ronald Duncan; "Organic," excerpts from F. L. Wright selected by Ralph Reid; "Albertus Magnus"; "The Poetics of Music" by Igor Stravinsky, edited by David Gordon.
>
> *Edge* 8: "David Lubin" by O. R. Agresti; "Pierrots" by Jules Laforgue; "In Praise of the *Kuan Tzu*."

FROBENIUS, LEO: German anthropologist, archeologist and explorer (1873–1938); authority on prehistoric art and culture, especially of Africa (to which he organized 12 expeditions between 1904–35); also dealt with living African cultures and folklore. Founded the Institute for Cultural Morphology (1922) in Frankfurt, which housed collection of prehistoric paintings and engravings. Author of *Erlebte Erdteile*, 7 vols. (1925–9). English translations of his works: *The Voice of Africa* (tr. 1913); *Prehistoric Rock Pictures in Europe and Africa* (1937); and *African Genesis*, ed. D. C. Fox (1983). Influenced work of Boris de Rachewiltz: *Black Eros* and *Introduction to African Art*, both translated by Peter Whigham (1964 & 1966). *Cf.* also Mary de Rachewiltz, "Pound and Frobenius."

References to Frobenius can be found throughout Pound's writings (esp. *The Cantos* and *Guide to Kulchur*). Pound cited *Erlebte Erdteile* as being more important than Frazer's *The Golden Bough*, and drew from Frobenius the germinal concepts of *Paideuma* and *Sagetrieb*. See *Il Liuto di Gassire*, trans. into Italian by Siegfried Walter de Rachewiltz (Milan: Scheiwiller, 1961), with Pound's "Significato di Leo Frobenius" [Gallup B70].

GESELL, SILVIO: (1862–1930), Minister of Finance of the second Munich Republic (1919); monetary reformer and author of *The Natural Economic Order*. His ideas concerning money, particularly stamp scrip, were influential on Pound's own economic ideas. See *Guide to Kulchur, Selected Prose* (esp. "The Individual in His Milieu," pp. 272–82), and the references to the Wörgl experiment with stamp scrip in *The Cantos*.

Giovannini, Giovanni: Professor of English at The Catholic University of America, Washington, D.C.; frequent visitor at St. Elizabeths. Author of "The Strange Case of Ezra Pound," *New Times* (August 26, 1955), pp. 194–6.

GOULLART, PETER: Russian born (c. 1900) traveller and writer. Author of *Forgotten Kingdom* (London: John Murray, 1955) which describes in detail the life and culture of the Na-Khi tribes of southwest China, "untouched by the complexities of modern life" (p. 218).

Pound discovered Goullart's *Forgotten Kingdom* in the summer of 1956. See Carroll F. Terrell, "The Na-Khi Documents I: The Landscape of Paradise," *Paideuma*, vol. 3, no. 1.

JUNZABURO NISHIWAKI: (1896–?) Japanese poet and scholar; wrote introduction to Ryozo Iwasaki's translation of Pound's "Mauberley." His poem "January in Kyoto" appeared in *Edge* 5. [It was also translated into Italian by Mary de Rachewiltz and published by Vanni Scheiwiller in 1959.]

Kuan Tzu: Lewis Maverick edited *Economic Dialogues in Ancient China: Selections from the Kuan-Tzu*, trans. T'an Po-fu and Wen Kung-wen (Carbondale, 1954). Kuan Chung (7th century B.C.) was the author of the *Kuan Tzu*; passages appeared in *Edge* 6, pp. 21–4.

LINNAEUS, CAROLUS: (1707–78), Swedish botanist; originator of modern scientific classification of plants and animals; author of *Systema naturae* (1735 & 1758); *Genera plantarum* (1737); *Species plantarum* (1753); et al.

For clarity of perception and lucidity of nuances of gradations, Linnaeus is placed by Pound alongside Mozart. See *Cantos* CXIII, CXV.

MAVERICK, LEWIS ADAMS: (1891–?); author of *China, A Model for Europe*, (San Antonio, 1946): vol. 1, *China's Economy and Government*; vol. II, *Despotism in China* (translation of François Quesnay's *Le Despotisme de la Chine*, Paris, 1767); also *Time Series Analysis* (San Antonio, 1945), an analysis of American business cycles, and how to forecast and control them. See also Kuan Tzu entry in Glossary.

MENCIUS: Meng-tse (371?–288? B.C.); Chinese Confucian philosopher. *The Book of Mencius* is considered one of the Four Books of the Chinese Classics (see Pound's *Confucian Analects*). Appalled by social anarchy, Mencius urged the rulers to practice the doctrines of Confucius. Central to his philosophy was the tenet that man is by nature good, and that his innate moral sense can be developed by cultivation or perverted by an unfavorable environment. Mencius held that the duty of a ruler is to ensure the prosperous livelihood of his subjects, and that warfare be eschewed except for defense. If a ruler's conduct reduces his subjects to penury, then he must be deposed. Proposed specific reforms in landholding and other economic matters.

  The Book of Mencius was described by Pound "as the most modern book in the world" ("A Visiting Card"). David Gordon's "Mencius" appeared in *Edge* 1.

ORAGE, A(LFRED) R(ICHARD): (1873–1934), socialist and journalist; publisher and editor of *The New Age* (London) and founder of *The New English Weekly*, journals which provided a forum for social, cultural and political criticism. Orage, as editor of these journals, provided Pound with a direct outlet for close to 300 articles, spanning 10 years (see Gallup).

  See Pound's "Obituary: A. R. Orage" and "In the Wounds," *Selected Prose*. See also the entry for C. H. Douglas in the Glossary.

ROCK, JOSEPH F.: Research Fellow (at the time), Harvard-Yenching Institute of Cambridge, Mass. Author of numerous works on the Na-Khi culture: *The Ancient Na-khi Kingdom of Southwest China*, 2 vols. (Harvard-Yenching Institute Monograph Series, vols. 8–9, 1947), and the *²Zhi ³Ma Funeral Ceremony of the Na-khi of Southwest China* (Studia Instituti Anthropos, vol. 9, Vienna, 1955). See especially his long article "The ²Muan ¹Bpo Ceremony or the Sacrifice to Heaven as Practised by the ¹Na-²Khi" (in *Monumenta Serica, Journal of Oriental Studies of the Catholic University of Peking*, vol. XIII, 1948, 1–160). See also Carroll F. Terrell, "The Na-Khi Documents I," *Paideuma*, vol. 3, no. 1, pp. 91–124.

THE SQUARE DOLLAR SERIES: published in Washington, D.C. by John Kaspar and David Horton, advertised itself as "American textbooks for students who want first things first," and included the following titles, each priced at one dollar: 1) *The Chinese Written Character as a Medium for Poetry* by Ernest Fenollosa, and (in the same volume) *The Unwobbling Pivot* and *The Great Digest* of Confucius, translated by Pound; 2) *The Analects* of Confucius, translated by Pound; 3) *Gists of Agassiz, or Passages on the Intelligence Working in Nature*, selected by Kaspar; 4) *A History of Monetary Crimes* by Alexander Del Mar; 5) *Bank of the United States* (from *Thirty Years' View*) by Thomas Hart Benton; 6) *Roman and Moslem Moneys* by Del Mar. [Kaspar and Horton also published Del Mar's *History of the Netherlands Monetary Systems* and *The History of Money in America*, as well as Eustace Mullins' *A Study of the Federal Reserve*.]

Described in *Edge* 6: "This set of books contains the minimum that will have to be added to any college curriculum, or, in part, required for college entrance, before the colleges can be regarded as caring for the education of their victims. Its philosophic or anagogic aim is to instil respect for the *intelligence working in nature* and requiring no particular theories to keep it alive: a respect that is reborn in a series of sages, from Confucius, through Dante, to Agassiz" (p. 28).

SWABEY, REVEREND HENRY: Anglican vicar of Louth in Lincolnshire; wrote on monetary reform, especially as it concerned Anglican Church. Editor of Social Credit paper *Voice*, to which Pound anonymously contributed; author of several articles appearing in *Edge*, and of "The Church and Usury." Translated Thaddeus Zielinski's *La Sibylle; see* letters of May 16 and 28, 1957. *See also* Swabey's "A Page without Which . . . ," *Paideuma*, vol. 5, no. 2, and Gallup C1590; "Towards an A.B.C. of History," *An Examination of Ezra Pound.*

VAN BUREN, MARTIN: (1782–1862), 8th president of the U.S. (1837–41); served as Secretary of State and Vice President under Andrew Jackson, to whom he acted as an advisor. As president, Van Buren, wary of the existing banking system, in order to deal with the economic crisis of 1837 backed the Independent Treasury System (established by Congress in 1840). Opposed the extension of slavery; was the presidential candidate of the Free Soil Party (1848); supported Lincoln during secession crisis. Author of *An Inquiry into the Origin and Course of Political Parties of the U.S.* (published posthumously in 1867), and *Autobiography* (1920).

See references to Van Buren in Carroll F. Terrell's *A Companion to the Cantos of Ezra Pound* (Berkeley: Univ. of California Press, 1980) and *Canto* XXXVII.

ZIELINSKI, THADDEUS: Polish professor of Greek, University of Warsaw; author of *La Sibylle, Trois Essais sur la Religion Antique et le Christianisme* (Paris: Redier, 1924). *La Sibylle* undertakes to differentiate Graeco-Christian religious thought from Judaism: the latter is opposed to the cult of beauty; to a plurality of gods; and to the union of God and man (*i.e.*, woman) in the begetting of messiahs (and/or demi-gods and heroes). "*C'est dans la religion antique que nous trouvons le veritable Ancien Testament de notre Christianisme*" (p. 125). *Edge* 2 was entirely devoted to a translation of *The Sibyl.*

W. C. Williams wrote of *Edge* 2: "It has opened a new world for me." Pound knew of *The Sibyl* prior to 1942 and held it in esteem as a central text for his agenda. *See also* the entry for Henry Swabey in the Glossary.

BLACK SWAN BOOKS
Literary Series

- [ ] H. D., *Hedylus*
- [ ] H. D., *Bid Me to Live*
- [ ] H. D., *Hippolytus Temporizes*
- [ ] H. D., *Ion*
- [ ] Ezra Pound / John Theobald,
  Letters
- [ ] Ezra Pound / Tom Carter,
  Letters
- [ ] Ezra Pound / Sen. Borah,
  Letters
- [ ] *Ezra Pound & Japan*
- [ ] Peter Whigham,
  Things Common, Properly
- [ ] Peter Russell,
  All for the Wolves
- [ ] Adrian Stokes,
  With All the Views
- [ ] W. B. Yeats, *Byzantium*
- [ ] Vernon Watkins,
  Unity of the Stream
- [ ] Ralph Gustafson,
  At the Ocean's Verge
- [ ] Peter Jones,
  The Garden End
- [ ] Michael Hamburger,
  Variations
- [ ] Lawrence Durrell, *The Ikons*
- [ ] D. H. Lawrence, *Ten Paintings*

Catalogue available

10-8/98   1 8/98